Learning to Dance
in the Rain

Learning to Dance
in the Rain

A True Story About Life Beyond Death

Lori & Brian McDermott

BALBOA.
PRESS
A DIVISION OF HAY HOUSE

ISBN: 978-1-4525-3713-9 (sc)
ISBN: 978-1-4525-3714-6 (e)
ISBN: 978-1-4525-3715-3 (hc)

Library of Congress Control Number: 2011913220

Balboa Press books may be ordered through booksellers or by contacting:

Balboa Press
A Division of Hay House
1663 Liberty Drive
Bloomington, IN 47403
www.balboapress.com
1-(877) 407-4847

Because of the dynamic nature of the Internet, any web addresses or links contained in this book may have changed since publication and may no longer be valid. The views expressed in this work are solely those of the author and do not necessarily reflect the views of the publisher, and the publisher hereby disclaims any responsibility for them.

The author of this book does not dispense medical advice or prescribe the use of any technique as a form of treatment for physical, emotional, or medical problems without the advice of a physician, either directly or indirectly. The intent of the author is only to offer information of a general nature to help you in your quest for emotional and spiritual well-being. In the event you use any of the information in this book for yourself, which is your constitutional right, the author and the publisher assume no responsibility for your actions.

Any people depicted in stock imagery provided by Thinkstock are models, and such images are being used for illustrative purposes only.
Certain stock imagery © Thinkstock.

Printed in the United States of America

Balboa Press rev. date: 08/09/2011

ജ *For Maia* ൽ

Contents

Preface

On February 20, 2010, a tragic car accident took the life of our twenty-one year old daughter, Maia. It was a personal earthquake, shattering our world and compelling us onto a very different life journey than the one we had been planning. *Learning to Dance in the Rain* chronicles the first year of this journey, the most heart-wrenching, difficult, yet spiritually uplifting period of our lives.

The pages you see before you are derived from an earlier version of *Learning to Dance in the Rain* which we distributed to family and friends in preparation for the first anniversary of Maia's death. At the time, the thought of publication was nowhere in sight. Our story, however, brought forth more positive feedback than we anticipated and we realized that sharing our experiences so openly was helping others continue to find comfort, healing, and spiritual growth, as well as ourselves. Additionally, many people encouraged us to "share it with the world" and after considerable discussion and research, we decided to take their advice.

We truly believe that sharing our story in this way is what our daughter would want us to do and we sincerely hope that our experiences will help others find inspiration and strength to face whatever dark times and challenges may come their way.

Acknowledgements

With some thoughtful editorial feedback from two of our friends, Pat Hammond and Nancy Brooks, the original manuscript underwent a few modifications to improve readability and understanding. We are deeply grateful to them and to another good friend, Chris Ebstein, who carved out time in her very busy schedule to help design the book's front and back covers.

We would also like to thank the many friends and family members who gave us permission to quote them, refer to them by name, and/or encouraged us throughout this project. They are too numerous to mention separately but we trust that they know who they are and that their love and support mean more to us than words could ever express.

Prologue

It was one of our worst imagined nightmares: The knock on the door and the words "there's been a very bad car accident." But this time it wasn't a dream – it was real.

We remember the events that followed in vivid detail: the questions we asked ("How bad an accident?" "Are you sure it was her?"), the refusal to accept such news without proof and driving in shock first to the scene of the crash, then on to the home of the friend we prayed she was still with, selfishly hoping someone else had been driving her car… Desperate banging on the door finally awoke those inside who, with puzzled expressions, told us, "No, Maia's not here. She decided not to sleep over and left for home a few hours ago."

The reality hit hard. In the cold dark air of that February morning the inconceivable became our truth. Our beloved daughter, our most cherished Maia, without any warning or apparent reason, was gone. Death had come while we were sleeping and taken her away. Her life was ended, her voice silenced. Maia would be no more.

Or so we thought. What we didn't fully appreciate at the time was that death is as much a beginning as it is an end, and that it is this way for both the soul, newly departed from its flesh and blood vessel, and for those of us left behind who struggle to adjust and find meaning.

What follows is a personal story, a chronicle of recovery and renewal describing how we, and many of our family members and friends, are learning to dance in the rain during one of the most painful storms life can give. It is a story we dedicate to our daughter, Maia Felisse, with endless love and gratitude for all she has taught us, and continues to teach us, about living life more consciously, with greater compassion, humor, and spirituality, and in constant wonderment of it all.

Days 1-7

Day 1

Faced with the inescapable reality of Maia's death, there was nothing else to do but go home. In the early dawn hours, we arrived back at the house and found ourselves on the threshold of a most unwelcome new world, a world we were utterly unprepared for and still unwilling to accept. Knowing there was no turning back, and with great sadness and heaviness of heart, we stepped over that threshold together.

Other families faced with a similar crisis might draw upon the beliefs and rituals of their religious affiliations and practices. What to do, when to do it, how to be and feel and think would be all laid out for them to follow. The immeasurable pain and grief would still exist, but there would be a clear path to guide them and a community of like-minded supporters to help them through the days ahead.

We, on the other hand, had no predetermined rituals or religious practices to lead us through such uncharted waters. Although born into Jewish and Christian families, we never fully embraced either tradition and when our own children were born, we tried adapting the teachings from many different religions to create a tradition of our own. The result was an eclectic, loosely defined spiritual belief system supported by two basic assumptions: the universe has both physical and non-physical attributes, and humans are both physical and spiritual beings. Great ideas that served us well in normal times, but lacking enough substance to be of immediate help during a crisis like this.

With daylight just barely breaking, we decided to delay calling the one person we knew could provide us with the spiritual and practical guidance now needed, our good friend Loni. While we waited, we gathered lots of photos of Maia, lit candles, and focused our thoughts on her. We didn't really know what to say or do, but we knew it was absolutely essential that we at least do something. Although her physical body had died, we believed her spiritual essence had not and that this part of her still needed us, perhaps more now than ever before. Working hard to put aside our own sense of loss and pain, and the myriad questions spinning through our heads, we sat together in silence, sending out thoughts of love and strength to our daughter, hoping with all our hearts that this would make a difference.

Phone calls were made, the news spread, and friends began to gather. One of our closest friends drove into Boston to pick up our son, Maia's only sibling and the only family member within easy traveling distance. As our numbers grew, we became a community of mourners, acutely aware of the need to support one another, draw strength from one another, and reach out to Maia in whatever ways we could. Representing a wide variety of religious backgrounds and spiritual beliefs, we were united in one mission: unconditional love and support for Maia and her transition from this life to whatever comes next.

One final detail worth noting: Earlier in the day as we were tidying the house for the visitors we knew would stop by, Lori picked up one of the many books lying around, Six-Word Memoirs. Opening it at random, she read in amazement the following quote: "The car accident changed my life." An extraordinary coincidence for sure, and the first of many we would experience in the days and months to come.

Day 2

We slept poorly that night, tossing and turning fitfully, waking up often, first at 2:20, exactly 24 hours after the reported time of Maia's death, then at 4, and 5, until finally we gave up on any more sleep and got out of bed.

The house was eerily quiet and strangely peaceful. Some of the candles from the day before were still lit so we sat silently in their warm glow and held each other close. Never before had we felt so much sadness and despair. And of course there were regrets. Although we still didn't know what caused Maia's crash, we wondered whether we could have said or done something that would have led to a very different outcome.

Admittedly, none of this self-admonishment would change the reality at hand. What was done could not be undone, and we had enough sense about us to know that this was not the time to focus on regrets. We had much more important work to do and we didn't yet know how or what this would entail.

With some time to spare before the day's wave of visitors would begin arriving, we turned on the computers to check email. Though others might expect email messages to be a poor way to exchange sentiments during such a time as this, we found them to be otherwise and were very comforted by the many that had begun to arrive. One of the most consoling and encouraging notes came from an uncle in California who wrote: *"I hope that Maia will make her presence felt to you, or to someone (we don't know the logic of such events), and that you will be able to feel something of her life and destiny on the other side of death."* Consoling, encouraging, and prophetic.

The day progressed with a flurry of activity. Many friends stopped by to offer whatever support they could and to be with us during this most difficult of times. Food, drinks, and all the required table settings seemed to appear out of nowhere, as did beautiful flower arrangements, candles, and plants. Our good friend Loni, who graciously accepted the role of spiritual leader and seemed quite comfortable with our rather non-traditional spiritual/religious inclinations, worked hard to provide us with a variety of resources to help us forge our own path through the days to come.

After taking her advice to secure the services of a local funeral director, Loni guided us in planning brief evening ceremonies at the house, an adaptation of the Jewish tradition of sitting shiva. At first we were somewhat reluctant to receive guests at night because in many ways we just wanted to be alone. But soon it became apparent that these gatherings were not primarily for us or for the many people who mourned Maia's death with us. They were most importantly for Maia. "Where a person lived, there does his spirit continue to dwell," a belief common to many religious and spiritual traditions, became our belief and one of our strongest guiding principles. Although we hadn't yet felt her presence in any tangible way, we knew deep inside that she was still with us. We might not be able to see or feel or hear her, but we could love her and be here for her, and that's what mattered most.

Day 3

It is often said that bad news travels on wings and a thousand leagues away, and so it was with this bad news. By Monday it seemed like the whole world knew of Maia's death.

The cyberspace grapevine was doing its thing. Facebook, email distribution lists, online newspapers, and the newly created page for Maia on the funeral home website were connecting countless people who were somehow linked to Maia and/or to us. Condolences, offers of support, and wonderful stories of how Maia made a difference to someone/somewhere/somehow began to arrive in waves.

It was all reassuring yet painfully heart wrenching at the same time. Our daughter, who led one of the most socially driven lives of all the young adults we knew in her peer group, often complained to us that few people cared about her the way she cared about them, that while she would go above and beyond to help any of her friends, only a few were ever there for her. As her parents, we would listen and try to soothe such melancholy moments, encouraging her to focus on the many positive relationships we knew she had. Now, according to the testimonies we were receiving, it seemed that Maia was more loved and admired than we could ever have imagined and we cried in sorrow that she may have died not knowing just how much she meant to so many people.

Along with the outpouring of love and consolation, more details of her final hours began to emerge.

Lori: "When I had last spoken with her, on Friday at about 5:30 p.m., Maia was happily on her way to Worcester with plans to have some fun with a longtime friend. The intent was to shop and have dinner, enjoy some time with her friend's family, and then hit the clubs for a 'girls' night out.' Maia assured me that this would be an especially meaningful visit since her friend had not been out much since giving birth last year. To cap off this impromptu jaunt, she planned to sleep over and then drive with her friend and the baby to our home in Clinton for an afternoon visit."

Although Maia sounded fairly upbeat on the phone and we knew it would be great to see her the next day, we both wished that she had just stayed put at school for the weekend. Mostly we were concerned that this trip was another example of her burning the candle at both ends. But we were also concerned about her partying with the hometown crew in central Massachusetts as her reputation for attracting social drama was particularly polished in this area of the state. Hoping for the best, and not wanting to plant any seeds of doubt or misgiving, Lori wished her a good night and said, "OK, have fun, see you tomorrow."

As it turned out, "girls' night out" ended in major social drama, not only with her good friend but apparently also with a guy she had expected to connect with. Angry words were exchanged between Maia and this young man, and soon after between Maia and her friend. We're not sure if the couple of drinks they had during their three hours at the club contributed to the escalation of emotions, or if some of the frustrations she was experiencing at school primed her for a confrontation, but whatever the cause, Maia left her friend's house in a swirl of agitation. Five minutes later, her car crashed into the pole.

We may never know for sure what actually happened to cause such a horrific accident. Emotional distress and excessive speed are the only two indisputable factors, with alcohol or some other compromising circumstance perhaps playing a role. But, again, we do not know anything else with certainty and in the long run, emotional distress and excessive speed may be the only ones that really matter.

Day 3 ended with extreme lamentation: Why, why, why did this happen to Maia? Why did her young life have to end? Is there something we could have done differently that would have changed the fate time had rendered? Is there something anyone could have done? If there is some higher lesson, meaning or purpose that we are to take from this, please, someone, anyone, let us know for all we have right now is deep, deep despair, unfathomable emptiness, and inexhaustible grief.

Day 4

Tuesday morning greeted us with a bright blue sky and unusually mild temperatures. Despite these favorable conditions, tension and anxiety filled the air in anticipation of an 8:30 a.m. appointment at a Worcester crematorium. It was there that we would be within inches of Maia's physical remains and say our last good-byes.

Our soft-spoken funeral director, Tom, picked us up at 8 and drove us into Worcester. While he and our son chatted about school and music on the way down, we sat silently in the back. In our laps we held each others' hands and a few cherished mementos we thought should be with Maia during the cremation process: a recent photo of the four of us, one of her first baby blankets, the "Happy 'Birth' Day" t-shirt she had received from the staff at St. Joseph Hospital on the day she was born, a copy of the poem her grandfather had written for her to celebrate her birth, and two pink and yellow roses, important symbols of Maia's life.

Tom, the three of us, and the kindly crematory operator were the only ones present to witness our solemn and simple ceremony. A moment or two to catch our breath at the sight of the six foot long cardboard casket with the hand written word "Head" at one end; perhaps three or four minutes of silent, tearful communion, our hands touching the casket's surface on sections where we thought her head and heart might be; and then the joint effort of the three of us to roll the casket into the cremation chamber, release the lever to close the door, and push the button that would start the chamber's heat. Another long, silent minute or two, and then we were done.

The ride home was less tense and perhaps more quiet – we really can't remember if Sean and Tom continued their conversation or not. Arriving back home around 9:30, Tom let us out at the bottom of our driveway. As we walked up, Lori was the first to notice an unusual gathering of birds in one of the back yard maple trees – blue jays! We watched in awe as at least 20 jays ruffled their wings, fluttered from branch to branch, and softly squawked amongst themselves. Why they had gathered, in this tree, at this time, we knew immediately – Maia. How they had come to be like this and what message we were to receive from their assembly, we were not sure. Regardless, our hearts filled with momentary joy and wonder.

Later in the day we were heartened to find the following information on the internet describing the significance of blue jays from a Native American perspective. Although we were still not sure how they had come together or the exact message that was intended, we clearly felt that these jays had brought us a gift of immeasurable worth.

Air Animal Totems:
Soaring to New Heights of Understanding

Air Animal Totems have a penchant for assisting us in matters of higher knowledge. Air being the most ethereal of elements, it's understandable that the creatures who inhabit it are able to lend the best understanding of its invisible ways. Closest to the heavens, air animals are our best allies as they herald our desires to the very gods in the skies.

Air animal totems are also symbols of strength (both physical and mental) and sovereignty. Very important traits, particularly when we are experiencing new transitions or surroundings in our lives. If air animal totems are catching your attention, you should feel very heartened by their presence. Allow their spirit to boost your confidence, and remind you that the ultimate power is within this present, unseen moment. Air animals are good omens, and their appearance is like a wink from god.

By Avia Venefica
http://www.whats-your-sign.com/air-animal-totems.html

Blue Jays

Blue Jay *reflects lessons in using your own power properly; as well as not allowing yourself to be placed in a position in which power is used against you. The word "jay" comes from the Latin "gaia" or "gaea" - Mother Earth. In Greek mythology the union of Mother Earth (Gaea) and Father Heaven (Uranus) resulted in the first creatures who had the appearance of life. This ability is reflected in the jay's ability to link heaven and earth; to access each for greater power. The blue jay as a totem can move between both heaven and earth and tap into the energies of both.*

The crest on the jay's head is symbolic of higher knowledge that can be used when focused. It is a reminder that to wear the crown of true mastership requires dedication, responsibility and committed development in all things in the physical and spiritual. Jay is a reminder to follow through on all things - do not start something then leave it dangling while you fly off for the next thing that sparkles and catches your fancy.

Blue jay reflects that a time of greater resourcefulness and adaptability is about to unfold. The jay does not usually migrate so use this as a reminder that there will be ample time to develop and use your energies to access new levels. It will stay around and work with you as long as you need it.

The blue jay is actually a member of the crow family and most crows have no fear. Crows and jays will group together and mob hawks and owls to drive them off. The jay is fearless and this can be of assistance to you to connect with the deepest mysteries of the earth and the greatest of the heavens.

Blue jays have a tremendous ability for survival with the least amount of effort. They reflect great talent. However, that talent must be developed and utilized properly. When jay shows up in your life it signals a time that you can begin to develop the innate royalty that is within you, or simply be a pretender to the throne. It all depends on you. The jay will teach you either way.

By Lucinda (adapted from Animal-Speak, by Ted Andrews)
http://turtlezen.com/bluejay.html

Day 5

Feeling like we never really slept, we awoke to Wednesday bleary eyed and exhausted. The strain of the previous four days was beginning to wear on us and we lingered in bed as long as we could.

Staring out the window at tree branches glistening with newly fallen snow, we talked a little about what the day had in store. Yesterday's finalizing of the Memorial Service date, time, and location meant that several very time sensitive tasks were at hand: selecting photos and music for a tribute video; organizing the order of service and designing the program; contacting a caterer to take care of food during the reception to follow; helping to make transportation/ lodging arrangements for family members who were starting to arrive; and on and on and on. Our heads were spinning with the thought of it all and our hearts were too broken to care.

As our thoughts drifted back to the previous morning and the miraculous gathering of blue jays, we were struck anew by the tremendous mystery and power surrounding us. Our past personal encounters with death (parents, grandparents, aunts, uncles, cousins, and one brother-in-law who, sadly, we did not have enough time to get to know well) provided little preparation for what we were now experiencing. In a way we wished we had some spiritual guru to clearly show us the path but we knew that on this journey, while others could share their thoughts and advice, there was no one to take the reins but us. And somehow we also knew that if we continued to keep Maia at the center of all our decisions, we would get through the next few days well enough.

The sound of a plow and scrape of a shovel roused us into action. Unbeknownst to us, an invisible network of support had arranged for some able bodied neighbors to clear our driveway and sidewalks of the newly fallen snow. Of course, this was not the first time, nor the last, we would find ourselves grateful for the unconditional outpouring of concern shown to us, and the love shown to Maia, by an ever-growing circle of friends. We had not known the full meaning of community until now and often found ourselves humbled by, and in awe of, its power and goodness.

The first blood relatives, Lori's sister and one of her brothers, two of Maia's closest aunts and uncles, arrived later that day. Meri and Mitch had known and loved Maia since she was a baby, and had recently spent some wonderful quality-time with her at Meri's Bat Mitzvah celebration in Sedona just two months before. No one would have thought then that our next gathering would be for her funeral...

The house was fairly full that night as Loni led another evening ceremony of song, prayer, and candle lighting for Maia. Simultaneously across the state in Amherst, in one of the UMass assembly halls, three hundred of Maia's classmates and friends gathered together to mourn her death and celebrate her life...the power and goodness of community humbling and amazing us again.

Day 6

Thursday dawned with another full agenda and preparation for the next wave of family members to arrive. From as far as the Pacific coast and as near as New York, siblings, aunts, uncles, cousins, and both of Brian's parents, were planning to come. Unfortunately, a crazy storm system was pushing its way up the Atlantic coast causing travel plans for a few people to be either delayed or cancelled. It was one more thing to worry about and we just hoped everyone on the road or in the air would arrive safely.

Although most of the Memorial Service decisions had been made and were now out of our hands, one of the most important details remained: what the three of us, Maia's parents and only sibling, were going to say. Earlier in the week when we first started thinking about what to include in the service, we immediately agreed that each of us would prepare something to read. Even though we knew it could be difficult to speak in front of a church full of people during such an emotional event, we felt we had no choice. We were her parents and brother, she was our daughter and sister, and this ceremony would be the most important opportunity we would have to show her just how much she meant to us.

While Sean seemed able to put together his thoughts with relative ease, we labored for days over what to say. Finally, when the last revisions were made, we began to practice reading them aloud. Lori soon discovered that her voice cracked and her eyes teared every time. It was apparently going to be a real struggle for her to get through so we asked her sister to be prepared to "stand in" for her if needed. Meri agreed without hesitation.

By 4:00 p.m., our many other out-of-town relatives began arriving. Although we were bracing ourselves for highly emotional and grieving receptions, tearful hugs of greeting soon turned into semi-light hearted and love-filled speculations about where and how Maia might be now. What a pleasant discovery to learn that several of our family members believed Maia was not "gone" but "transformed" and that as heart breaking as it was for her not to be with us in flesh and blood, she would still be with us, and tangibly so, in spirit. This was so what we needed to hear.

As the evening progressed, the weather turned wild and the skies poured more rain than we had seen in a really long time. Undeterred, our family and friends arrived in large numbers and the house soon filled for the last evening of prayer, song, and sharing for Maia. The presence of so many family members created a palpable change in the flow and feel of energy throughout the house and so, with a thunderous winter storm raging outside, the love and communion occurring inside made that night's gathering the most emotional and powerfully moving we had yet to experience. And no doubt about it, Maia was present, in a form we could neither see nor hear, but one we knew was surrounding us all.

Day 7

Friday, the day we had been simultaneously planning for and deeply dreading, had arrived. With weighted hearts and exhausted bodies, we began preparing for what we knew would be the most significant and emotional event of our 24 year marriage – the 4:00 p.m. gathering of family and friends to commemorate and celebrate the life of our beloved Maia.

Lori: "Having already decided what to wear, the process of getting dressed was mercifully mindless. At the last minute, however, I decided that I needed to wear something of Maia's. I walked into her room and carefully began looking through her clothing and jewelry for something that would be appropriate. Admittedly, this was a very heartbreaking task so after about ten minutes of searching and not finding anything that felt right, I gave up my quest. Turning to leave the room, my head hit one of Maia's dangling knickknacks, causing me to shift position. As I did so, my gaze fell upon a necklace hanging from a hook on a small shelf. A black chain, a few clear beads, and a little silver pendant engraved with the letter 'M' … Perfect."

We were dressed by 10:00 and ready for the first difficult appointment of the day – meeting with Tom at the funeral home to have a few quiet minutes with Maia's ashes before he would transport them to the church. Tom had arranged the engraved wooden urn, a few framed photos of her and us, and one enlarged poster-size photo of Maia in a fashion that would be similar to their layout in the church later that day – so very sad, yet so very beautiful… and still so hard to accept.

Back at the house, family members began gathering and a few out-of-town friends stopped by for a little one-on-one time. Again as if out of nowhere, food was laid out in the dining room and anyone who wanted could grab a quick bite.

By three o'clock, all our relatives had gathered. Directions were shared, carpool teams were arranged, and everyone headed out to the church. All was going well until we came to an impassable section of road, flooded by a nearby river that had risen three feet from the previous night's torrential downpour.

Brian: "A local police officer was directing traffic and I had to get out of our car to talk with him to be sure that he would allow the entire eight car caravan to stay together. I remember thinking how strange it was to have this 'normal' discussion about trying to solve a traffic problem in contrast to the real event that was unfolding, and how finding the balance between the 'old normal' and the 'new normal' would probably be a constant challenge forever more."

The police officer was extremely accommodating. With his help we were able to make a slow but steady U-turn, arriving at the church without any further delay.

Tom invited us to gather in a large parlor behind the church sanctuary and it was there that we saw the printed Memorial Service programs for the first time. Maia's name on the front cover with two pink roses, a photo of her on the left inside page and the order of service on the right, and on the back cover the final quote Maia had posted on her Facebook page: "When life gives you a storm, dance in the rain." These ten little words, posted by Maia less than six weeks earlier in response to some frustrating situations she was dealing with at school, had become the new motto for our lives.

With plenty of time before the service was to begin, Tom asked if we would like to see how everything was arranged in the church sanctuary. We agreed and were completely awed by what we saw. Unlike our first visit a few days ago when this early 1800s church felt cold, dark, dusty, and bleak, today the sanctuary was warm, glowing, and welcoming, just what we had hoped it would be.

Back in the parlor, everyone was quietly chatting amongst themselves, making the most of this impromptu family reunion and reconnecting with each other's lives. At five minutes to four, Tom asked Loni to round us up before beginning our procession into the sanctuary. In unusually quick fashion, thirty-eight of us formed a silent circle around Loni. She had us take a few deep breaths, think about Maia, and then provided a few instructions regarding what was to take place.

Lori: "As soon as Loni finished talking, I remember feeling the need to introduce her to those who were not at our house the previous night and probably had no idea who she was. As I joined her in the circle's center, I remember putting my arms around her and explaining that she was one of our closest friends, a cantor at the Clinton synagogue, and that we could not thank her enough for being our spiritual guide during the past six days of sadness and uncertainty, and for helping us support Maia in her transition from this life to whatever comes next.

Then I remember turning toward Loni, looking intensely into her eyes, and saying something like, 'and I KNOW Maia is OK and is in a good place.' Then I remember speaking clearly and confidently to everyone, rotating slowly around the circle, my own eyes gazing deeply, powerfully into every other pair of eyes, saying something like, 'This will be a time to think about and remember Maia. There will be tears and sadness, but there will also be joy because we are here to honor and celebrate her life and amazing things will happen.' It really was as if someone else was speaking through me and I clearly remember saying two things as I headed back to my place between Brian and Sean: 'That was easy' and then, with a quick shudder through my body, 'Where did that come from?'"

Everyone seemed slightly stunned by Lori's uncharacteristic "take control" moment but there was no time to dwell on what had just happened. Tom was giving instructions on how to line up for our entrance into the sanctuary and the start of the service.

We entered to a standing room only crowd of Maia's friends and their families, our friends and colleagues, Sean's friends from childhood, high school, and college, and others who were in some way connected to our daughter. Later we would learn that an estimated 700 people were in attendance, vastly exceeding our expectations and completely overwhelming us with the realization that Maia's life had touched so many people so deeply.

Lori: "Right after we were seated in our pew and waiting for everyone else to get settled, I had this weird feeling of heightened expectation and excitement. I remember thinking, 'this is a *Being John Malkovich* moment' and feeling as if 'someone' (Maia?) had entered my head and was using me for a body. I remember looking around to see who was here and thinking, 'oops, don't look too happy; hunch your shoulders, look a little sad.' For the entire service, up until the Mourner's Kaddish at the end, I felt this 'Maia presence' with me and I think that is why I was able to be so strong and composed and at peace with how it all unfolded. I didn't even have any trouble reading what I had prepared – my voice was perfectly clear and steady."

One of Brian's cousins, Darren, sent out a beautifully written summary of the service and events that followed, which we include here because there is nothing more we would add:

The service was an event of unimaginable grief and, in a strange way, beauty. As always, Maia filled the room – in this case, three times over. She filled it with her presence, she filled it with something like 700 people who came to express their love for her and their pain in losing her, and she filled it again as many, many of those people walked up to the altar and told a story or offered a memory.

It was not a service designed to make things easier for anyone in the short term. There were no platitudes, no easy answers, no attempt to minimize or evade the grief. Before it began, the extended family members gathered in a waiting room and at one point stood in a circle for a powerful moment of silent reflection. Then Lori stepped into the circle and, spinning slowly around, looked each one of us in the eye. We would weep, she told us. But we would also celebrate Maia's life. And "amazing things" would happen, she said. And she was right.

We watched a slideshow of Maia's life. We chanted Maia's name, hundreds of voices echoing in a round inside the church. We heard Lori, Brian, and Sean describe their love for her, their memories of her, their indescribable pain at losing her. Uncle John (Maia's grandfather) read a beautiful poem he had written on the occasion of Maia's birth. We heard stories from neighbors, elementary school classmates, college roommates, friends from everywhere. Many, many people whose lives Maia had touched with her generosity, warmth and selflessness. Several people noted with certainty that the snow pouring down outside was Maia speaking to us. One man told how he met Maia standing on line behind her at a Verizon store. He was so blown away by how she took apart the difficult customer service clerk that he hired her on the spot.

Anyone who wanted to speak was welcomed. And when it was over, Sean and Brian and Lori stood for two hours receiving the hugs and the tears of those hundreds of people, clearly exhausted and just as clearly bathing in the love all these people had for Maia. They looked like the people in a movie who get shot with a bow and arrow or a bullet in the heart, and then stand there for what seems like an unrealistic amount of time, staring at you with wonder and confusion as the waves of pain wash over them.

I guess when something totally incomprehensible like this happens you have two basic choices: you can try to box it in, bottle it up, crawl under a rock and never come out, wrap yourself in the Hallmark sentiments at hand. Or you can dive in, believing that the only way to move forward is to try to comprehend what the Universe is up to. How could it be that this bright, shining light has been taken from us – or, what do we do now that it has happened?

Brian and Lori are diving in deep. They are finding meaning in Maia's life and her extraordinary ability to connect with people, the lessons she taught them and is still teaching them, and I think they have some thoughts about the journey that Maia's spirit is now undertaking.

So the service wasn't designed to be easy. But it was designed to be a step, a big step, in moving forward. Once the hundreds made their way through the receiving line, the crowd at the church function room started to thin out a bit. Some of Brian and Lori's dear friends broke out guitars and started playing and singing. Sean joined on mandolin and guitar for a bit, and Brian pulled out the harmonica for a few. Music for Maia, haunting and holy. But also a tiny step back into doing the things they love, normal things, which they must continue to do.

A bunch of family and close friends from the community went back to Brian and Lori's, ostensibly for just a quick visit. A few hours later, a core crew was still gathered in the kitchen. There was some beer, and some Bushmills. We picked at a platter of pickles and olives. There was amazing singing, a poem read aloud, and laughing, and lots more crying. It went late into the night.

Brian and Lori and Sean are not alone in this. And they don't want to be alone. They have an incredible set of friends surrounding them in Clinton and Boston. All of Brian and Lori's siblings were there, and many of their nieces and nephews. All of Brian's aunts and uncles. Cousins of all three. They talked a lot about their family, how important it is to them and how they want to keep in close contact with us. We talked about trying to do another McDermott family reunion this summer.

At the service, I talked about how Maia shone so brightly at Mary's party last summer. Many of us hadn't seen her in a long time, and she had become a beautiful young woman. She was charming, but not in a deliberate or self-conscious way. Every time I turned around she was talking or laughing with someone else. In talking with a lot of you since her death, everyone mentioned their vivid memories from that party. Hold those close. And please share them in a letter or phone call with Brian and Lori; I know that they would love to hear them.

Sending you all a ton of love. And a reminder to you: the tattoo that Maia wore, and the message the people of Clinton have painted on a giant boulder on the edge of town: Carpe Diem (Seize the Day).

Love,
Darren

Clinton's memorial rock painted for Maia.

A New Chapter Begins

2/27

The dawn of the eighth day marked the beginning of another phase in this new journey that had started for us on 2/20 at 2:20. Almost as if the previous seven days were a cocoon of time in which all we needed to do was focus on Maia and her transition (to what, we were still not sure), it was now time to emerge and face a totally upended world and a future that had shifted 180 degrees. Maia would remain number one on our minds, of course, but we needed to begin figuring out how to relate to this most unanticipated and still painful reality.

With the Memorial Service behind us, we were able to relax a little and appreciate the remaining time we had with the last few out-of-town family members and friends. Lori's sister had left early but not before the two of them created a spontaneous end-of-shiva ceremony to accompany the removal of the black shawls which had covered the downstairs mirrors. Simple, brief, and from the heart, they sent loving thoughts to Maia and, borrowing from Loni's Memorial Service introduction, promised to continue to reach out to her "through the porous veil separating where we are now from where you are now" and to continue to support her soul in its journey.

Later that morning, we found a few things outside our front door that had been delivered sometime during the night: two photo collages made by Maia's UMass roommates and a CD with "Maia's Song," a beautiful song written and produced by one of her classmates, Giddens Rateau. Seeing the photos of Maia having lots of fun with her UMass friends was very bittersweet. Surrounded by friends, carefree and happy – it was still so hard to accept that these times were ended forever. Listening to "Maia's Song," a beautiful tribute to her friendship with Giddens and the impact that her laughter and energetic personality had on those around her, was sad but hopeful as well. Two of the song's phrases, "she lives through us" and "let's celebrate her life from night til morning" became favorite and often repeated refrains.

As friends and family members stopped in to say good-bye, there was a lot of talk about the Memorial Service and how remarkable it all was, and about how amazing Maia was to generate such a powerful outpouring of love and caring. One of Brian's uncles, wondering aloud, speculated that perhaps this was her purpose in life, to make connections and spread love.

We talked also about the crash itself, how we may never know what actually happened, and how that doesn't really matter now. What does matter is how people remember Maia and are inspired by her, how we honor her life and celebrate her spirit, and how we keep our minds open to the myriad ways we can connect with her through that "porous veil." Being able to connect with those who have died was something we used to think might be possible but, if it was, it would only be possible for a very small population of uniquely gifted individuals. Even then we were not without a healthy dose of skepticism. Now, however, faced with a world with Maia either "dead and gone" or "dead and with us still," and already having a few astounding signs that the physical and spiritual worlds are intertwined and mutually accessible to one another, we were ready to do whatever was needed to stay connected. As it turned out, just being open to the possibility was a good start.

For example, earlier that morning we had decided it would be good to let everyone hear "Maia's Song" but hadn't figured out when would be the best time. Ultimately, the time was decided for us. As Lori was talking with Brian's brother, she realized he would be heading out in about a half hour. Taking a quick look at her cell phone, she gasped out loud: "11:11, that's Maia's time! We should play the song now." Indeed, whenever Maia was aware of 11:11 on a digital clock, she would stop and make a wish. We're still not sure where she picked up this tradition but it happened a lot to her and she would always make a big deal about it.

So it was that then and there, with about 25 friends and family members in the house, we played "Maia's Song." The power of that song, at that moment in time, deeply touched everyone and neither one of us could have planned it any better.

During the day we heard from quite a few of our friends who had been profoundly inspired by the Memorial Service and had some wonderful stories to share with us. Here are just a few:

From Kim: "*When I first heard that Maia had died, I saw her in a vision – shimmering, sparkling, happy, and totally at peace. At the Memorial Service, I could feel her presence fill the church.*"

From Nancy: "*As my husband and I were looking for a place to park our car before the Memorial Service on Friday, I randomly opened a book that was in my lap. On the page I opened was an excerpt from* The Prophet, *by Kahlil Gibran. I had never heard of him before and had a little time to begin reading the passage which started, 'Speak to us of Children. And he said, Your children are not your children…' You can imagine my astonishment, Lori, when you read aloud that very same excerpt during the service!"*

From Laurie: "The chant of Maia's name has been echoing at the top of my mind since your truly lovely service. Jim and I really felt her presence and spirit all around us, as we continue to hold you in our hearts and prayers. I woke up this morning with Maia Felisse singing in my head."

From Paul: "Karen got up before me and opened the blinds. Clouds still covered the sky and snow covered the trees in the woods out back, a place we have always felt is mystical and sacred. When I got out of bed a few minutes later I had the chant 'Maia, Maia' running through my head. I looked out and a single ray of sunlight broke through the clouds and shone on this lone crow sitting at the top of the tallest pine. The sunbeam disappeared in a few seconds. The crow remained long enough for me to grab my camera, called and then flew off."

Ever so slowly we were beginning to see how we might survive in this new, post-220 world: continue to celebrate Maia's life, continue to find ways to let her live through us (and through others who cared about and loved her), and purposefully commit ourselves to developing a greater understanding and awareness of life's non-physical/spiritual dimensions.

Although these strategies would not erase the pain and sorrow of being deprived of our beloved Maia and the joy, companionship, and energy of her physical self, we were hopeful that at the very least we would not have to resign ourselves to only memories and artifacts. Our recently renewed acquaintance with religious and spiritual traditions that accept the continuation of life after death, and our own unusual experiences to date, validated a growing belief that our relationship with Maia would continue in some way and in some form. But we did not really know how this was to happen. We had so many questions and still so very much to learn.

3/2

Despite our newly awakened awareness of "life after life" interactions, we were not yet able to rationalize away the pain of losing Maia physically and had a lot of agonizing moments ahead of us. One of the most heart-wrenching of all involved making that first trip back to her apartment at UMass. Although her roommates had told us that there was no rush to remove her belongings, we knew we needed to start the process and made arrangements to drive out today.

We arrived in the early afternoon and were warmly greeted by all three roommates. Hugs, tears, a few remarks about the Memorial Service (which they had lovingly contributed to with wonderful stories about Maia, her friendship with them, and some of their crazy college escapades), and then we went up to her room.

When we opened the door and saw all of her things arranged as if in a state of permanent suspended animation, tears fell from our eyes and our hearts filled with sorrow. The still incomprehensible reality of it all hit us again: Maia's not coming back to finish reading that book by the bed, or go to the next class on her schedule, or use her computer to send us an email, or cuddle with all those pillows, or ... Maia's not coming back at all.

As much as we were totally convinced about Maia's continuing spiritual presence, the pain of her being forever gone from this physical here and now world was unbearable. And so it was with tremendous sorrow and heartache that we sorted through some of her clothes and books and gadgets, packed up our car, and headed back to Clinton.

On the drive home, Brian was at the wheel and somehow managed to take a wrong turn. At least we thought it was a wrong turn until we realized that it brought us exactly where we needed to be. Here is his account of what happened.

Brian: "Lori and I are traveling back from UMass after going through Maia's belongings in her apartment. We take a back road and get kind of lost and end up on dirt roads and I'm driving a bit fast. Finally we come out on the road we need to be on. But there is no speed limit sign and so I'm driving faster than I should and speed past a police car. The lights start flashing and we are pulled over. I explain to the officer that I hadn't seen a speed limit sign but he takes my license and registration anyway and goes back to his car. I thought of how Maia was always able to 'talk her way' out of tickets and usually just get warnings. Just then I notice right in front of us is the number 20, Maia's number, on a little green sign. The policeman comes back and gives me a warning without my saying anything and asks me to watch my speed. I can just hear Maia saying, 'Chill Pops, take it easy… it's all going to be OK.' It was an easy leisurely drive the rest of the way home."

What might seem like a meaningless coincidence to others was for us another sign of Maia's continued presence. The number 20, which three weeks earlier had astoundingly struck us as a new "lucky" number when it appeared in striking fashion on three separate occasions during a weeklong trip to Florida, had now become not really so lucky in the traditional sense, but definitely powerful – Maia crashing her car at 2:20 on 2/20/2010 followed by the estimated 20 blue jays in our tree was just the beginning of a series of significant encounters with this number.

We still did not know what it all meant, but we were intent upon learning as much as we could. One thing we did feel pretty certain of: Maia's death had propelled us onto the most painful, sorrowful, awe-inspiring, mind-blowing, and spiritually enigmatic journey we would probably ever take.

Sunday was planned to be a day of rest before trying to resume our regular work schedules on the 8th. It was a beautiful day so we headed out for a walk along one of our favorite trails down by the Nashua River. Being outside, away from people and obligations, surrounded by woods, weeds, water, and sky seemed like just the therapy we needed.

Conversation, of course, centered on Maia and how much we loved and missed her. Questions abounded: Why did this all happen the way it had? Where is she, how is she, right now? What are we to do and how do we go on?

The events of the previous two weeks had brought us to a somewhat paradoxical state. On the one hand, we were absolutely devastated by the tragic and still incomprehensible finality of her death, and a future without her was something we could not as yet bear to even imagine. At the same time, however, we were tremendously uplifted by the outpouring of support for her and the inspiring stories people were sharing with us about how she had made so many positive impressions on others' lives. Additionally, there were the countless good deeds, donations, and renewed relationships that were being made in her name or because of her example which would ripple out beyond this moment to benefit countless individuals for untold days to come. The power of all this, as Loni had said at the Memorial Service, was "awe-inspiring."

But these were not the only thoughts to keep us from falling into the ever-tempting chasm of despair. Equally consoling if not more so, were the many indications that our beliefs regarding the dual physical-spiritual nature of human existence were somewhat accurate and that a spiritual Maia still existed and existed in ways with which we could still connect and tangibly experience.

For some people these thoughts and experiences might be nothing more than wishful thinking. Others might consider them irreverent or religiously misdirected. And of course there were those who had no difficulty celebrating and accepting them as facts. For us, they were becoming mysterious truths that we wanted with our utmost desire to understand more fully.

As we walked along we came to one of the first turns of the trail. Here we stopped to build a little memorial cairn for Maia. Wanting to begin with four rocks to represent the four of us, Lori found three nice sized rocks of decreasing size and easily created a sturdy, well balanced pile. Brian, charged with finding the fourth rock, was quite excited to come across one that resembled the head of a turtle, another important Maia symbol. Unfortunately, this one was larger than the others and Lori had a most difficult time getting it to balance. All of a sudden, as if an invisible force had taken over, the turtle head rock found its balance. Lori described this moment as "the feeling you get when two magnets pull toward one another and connect."

A little further along we walked through an open field and paused for a moment along the river's edge. Looking upward we gazed in wonder as an eagle circled high above. Just then, as if on some silent cue, four deer emerged together from the edge of the forest. Gazing upon us for an intense couple of minutes, they held their positions like statues before turning in unison and disappearing into the thicket. Two rare sightings that we immediately hoped might hold some deeper meaning.

Back at the house, a little internet searching came up with the following information about the symbolism of eagle and deer from a Native American spiritual perspective:

The Eagle is a symbol of the zenith, a great reminder of your own ability to soar to great heights. Eagles are messengers from heaven and are the embodiment of the spirit of the sun. Its four-toed feet remind you to stay grounded even when soaring high. Its talons remind you to grasp the things of the earth. Its sharp beak shows you when to speak, how much, and how strongly.

This totem will show you opportunities and how to ride the winds to your benefit. Eagle people can live in the realm of the spirit yet still remain connected and balanced within the realm of the Earth. You must become much more than you ever dreamed possible.

By Lin
http://www.linsdomain.com/totems/pages/eagle.htm

Deer: From the deer we can learn that the gift of gentleness and caring can help us overcome and put aside many testing situations. Only love, both for ourselves and for others, helps us understand the true meaning of wholeness. Only when we move through life in the spirit of love for all beings can we melt the barriers that separate us from others, from other life forms, and from the beautiful mystery which is our own magical and spiritual gift.

Deer teaches us how to exert keen observation and sensitivity. Deer are in tune with nature and all it comprises. They are sacred carriers of peace and show those with this power animal how to open their hearts and love unconditionally. Deer has entered your life to help you walk the path of love with full consciousness and awareness, to know that love sometimes requires caring and protection, not only in how we love others, but also in how we love ourselves.

When a Deer totem enters your world, a new innocence and freshness is about to be awakened. New adventures are just around the corner and there will be an opportunity to express the gentle love that will open new doors for you.

By Ina Woolcott
http://www.shamanicjourney.com/article/6025/deer-power-animal-symbol-of-gentleness-unconditional-love

3/20

The one-month anniversary and the first day of spring arrived together. With the support and wise guidance of our dear friend Karen, we invited about 20 of our closest friends to a Maia Remembrance – Spring Equinox Celebration:

Maia's Spring Equinox
1 p.m., Saturday, March 20

In Roman Mythology, Maia Maiestas was an earth goddess. As with her Greek counterpart, the Roman Maia symbolized youth, life, rebirth, love, and sexuality. She was also held as the goddess of plants and spring. Maia, along with her six sisters in the Pleiades, has her own star in the constellation Taurus, near Orion the Hunter in the star cluster M 45. More than five times larger than our sun, Maia lies some 385 light years away from Earth.

1. ***Welcome / Smudging / Give-away Collection****: Each guest is asked to bring a small personal, object to be given away. Each give-away object brings with it the love, joys, sorrows, and hopes of its owner, which are then shared communally. In native traditions, a give-away is a ceremony in which a tribe member gives away some or all of his or her or possessions to clear out his or her life from the old things and to make room for new things and is often held around the time of a death. The give-away ceremony means remembering that all of life is a gift.*

2. ***Grounding Meditation****: This meditation will connect us to the earth and to Maia as we envision her transition.*

3. ***Introductions and Intentions /Locating Our Places in the Circle****: Guests may introduce themselves and state an intention. In native traditions, a circle gathering is representative of a medicine wheel. Each area of the wheel offers a connection to the natural world and opportunity for contemplation.*

4. ***Offering****: Guests may bring a written offering to be burned: Blessings, prayers, dreams, and more can be read aloud or just offered to the fire. Just as fire transforms wood into smoke and ash, so too does sacred fire transform pain, grief, and disharmony into joy, balance, and peace.*

When one offers prayers and a symbol of the issue to be healed into sacred fire, one is directly communicating with the divine.

5. **Yoga Releasing Stretch**

6. **Solar Meditation**

7. **Take-away**: *Each guest will select something from the give-away collection, joining us together beyond this day.*

The day was gloriously warm. Karen led the ceremony which offered a number of unforgettable moments to nurture our need to be healed and our growing appreciation for life's mysteries. Brian's poem offering to the sacred fire may have expressed best what many of us were feeling:

It can't be, it doesn't make sense
How can this be, she can't be gone
She was too strong, she knew the way
She can't be gone, we just started to play
Ok, ok, you're not here anymore
But how can that be, I need to know
There are too many signs
That say you are there
But there's just not enough to know just where
How can that be, I need to know
You can't just be gone
That I know

Afterwards, we enjoyed one another's company, shared food, drink, and music making, and toasted Maia often. Under a clear, star filled sky, we gathered closely together and listened to her song, each of us undeniably transformed in some way by the life, and now the death, of our Maia.

Eight days later, many of us gathered again in Allston, MA for the Maia McDermott Memorial Concert. Organized by Sean and some of his Northeastern University classmates, the concert featured performances by four local bands, including his own, Red Bellows. Proceeds from the event (over $850) went to The Home for Little Wanderers, a Boston-based organization that provides essential support for youngsters faced with a variety of challenges. It was another extraordinary event to honor and celebrate Maia's life, and many of us there felt an amazing energy during the Red Bellows set. Maiaspirit, for sure.

April

During the months of March and April, friends and family members continued to share with us heartfelt sympathies, tips for healing, and wonderful memories of Maia. The apparent impact she had made on so many lives continued to amaze us.

Also during this time, a number of new books entered our home (e.g., Rudolph Steiner's <u>Staying Connected</u>, Brian Weiss's <u>Many Lives, Many Masters</u>, Ted Andrews' <u>Animal-Speak</u>, and <u>The Idiot's Guide to Communicating With Spirits</u>), and many older books were taken off shelves to be reread (e.g., <u>Tibetan Book of the Dead</u>, <u>I Ching</u>, Vicki Noble's <u>Motherpeace</u>, and E.F. Schumacher's <u>A Guide for the Perplexed</u>).

We turned off the television and turned on to anything we could to help us forge our way through this new post-220 world. Our three most fundamental goals: 1) let Maia's enthusiasm for life and compassion for others live on through us; 2) stay connected with her in whatever form she now existed; and 3) nurture our growing sense of spirituality and awakening to life's possibilities.

Of course, the post-220 world still retained the entire pre-220 work world, which for Brian, as a school district superintendent, was practically all-consuming. Consequently, he barely had any time to read and reflect. Fortunately for Lori, her 35 hour/week job as an early childhood coordinator was very pleasant work with extremely supportive colleagues. It afforded her much more time for exploration and contemplation, and her now one year old practice of yoga provided additional and essential support.

Lori: "The more I read and the more I talked with others, the more open I seemed to become to a wider range of experiences. My dreams became unusually vivid and occurrences of meaningful coincidences increased. One of my first memorable dreams had a 'vision quest' quality to it. In the dream I was walking alone and came upon a figure lying prone on the ground. Nothing else was around and the figure was covered in a full length, hooded cloak. Slowly the figure started to turn toward me, revealing itself to be a cougar. Its gaze penetrated mine and then I woke up."

Here is what Ted Andrews writes about the Cougar in <u>Animal-Speak</u>:

"Keynote: Coming into Your Own Power ... If cougar has shown up in your life, it is time to learn about power. Test your own... Now it is time to assert... (but) remember that power can be asserted gently... The cougar can teach you how to bring out your power and fill your heart with it in a manner that will enable you to take charge of your life." (<u>Animal-Speak</u>, pgs. 259-260)

Lori: "About two weeks after the Cougar Dream, I had another equally memorable dream. I was with Maia (as a child) on a boat. The water was raging and she was playing close to the edge. At one point she started to fall in and I grabbed her foot. But she was too heavy for me to pull up. So I thought about trying to grab her clothing but figured it would probably rip. Not knowing what else to do, I took a deep breath and, summoning that inner, adrenaline rush strength I had often heard about, pulled her back into the boat. A little while later, she was playing along the edge again and, just like before, started to fall into the water. This time I just grabbed her foot and pulled her to safety without hesitation. Once inside the boat, she gave a quick shake, looked me right in the eye, and said, 'See, mom, it's easy: don't think. just do.' I loved it: 'Don't think. Just do.' Simple, direct, and now one of our most favorite mantras."

Lori also started experiencing more encounters with "synchronicity," a term coined by the reknowned psychoanalyst Carl Jung to describe events that are causally unrelated but occur together in a meaningful manner. Dr. Jung saw these kinds of events as an expression of a deeper order, a governing dynamic, underlying the whole of human experience. Two extremely meaningful synchronicities that occurred right after Maia's death were: randomly opening <u>Six-Word Memoir</u> to "The car accident changed my life" and unintentionally turning toward Maia's "M" necklace the morning of her Memorial Service.

Lori: "Another compelling synchronicity involved the book <u>You Can't Afford the Luxury of a Negative Thought</u>, given to us by our friend Karen. On a Friday afternoon (4/16), I was feeling very depressed and opened it randomly to a page with two different references to roses. One was a quote in which the author wondered aloud why she could never get a perfect limousine, but somehow could always get one perfect rose. The other was on choosing your perspective, that even in very tough situations, we have a choice: we can choose to see either a rose garden or a thicket of thorns; it really is up to us.

The timing of this 'random' message was perfect as Fridays had been tough for me. I tended to relive each one as if it were 2/19 all over again (remembering my last text message and phone call with Maia, imagining what she might have been doing as Friday turned into Saturday, and then contemplating a series of possible events leading to her death). It was a depressing weekly ritual by which I had been marking the passage of time.

The page I turned to was just the medicine I needed to stall the tailspin and get me to see the rose garden, not a thicket of thorns. As if the reference to roses (a powerful symbol we associate with Maia) and the advice of the text itself were not enough, Brian noticed that when you add 4/16 together, you get 20. Perhaps another sign from beyond the porous veil reaching out to us with lots of love and just a touch of humor."

As it turned out, we were not the only ones experiencing signs and synchronicities. Following are notes from two of Maia's good friends which Lori received in April:

From Meghann: "So, funny story. I am driving down Route 2 yesterday and all of a sudden there is a car driving the wrong way on the highway going probably 80 miles an hour heading straight for me. Last minute he swerves and sideswipes the car next to me, only having minimal damage. Then a song comes on the radio that makes me think of Maia. Thanks for giving me a great guardian angel. I know she was with me yesterday."

From Alycia: "First I just want to say how happy your little blurb on your profile makes me whenever I see it (learning to dance in the rain). I get so happy and start thinking about all the times Maia and I were the only crazy people running through puddles and everyone looked at us like we were crazy ...Well I just wanted to write to you and let both you and Brian know that I think about you both constantly. I really do keep you both, and Sean of course, in my prayers all day. ... Let me know of any signs you've gotten from Maia recently because I'm always on the look out too! I was so happy because the other day I was walking past the hallway and I saw her face in front of me clear as day walking toward me. It was so surreal, it was like a dream I didn't want to wake up out of and I just kept looking straight ahead caught in a dead stare. All of sudden I snapped out of it and it was the strangest feeling because I just felt like she was there. I told my friends about it and the more I told the story I realized she must be up there laughing at me because she was trying to freak me out. She always loved playing jokes on me and running up on me because I would never wear my glasses and could never see her until she was practically two feet from my face :)!"

The month of April included a much needed getaway to Cape Cod. We stayed in a little house owned by Brian's aunt and uncle which was nestled in a secluded grove of trees along the National Seashore in Truro. We brought with us some food and wine, hiking shoes and binoculars, a few books and candles, a box of incense, and a small framed photo of Maia. It turned out to be the perfect place to unwind and reflect on all that had occurred in our lives during the past two months.

On the first morning we broke out Lori's 20-year-old set of Motherpeace tarot cards and her even older copy of the I Ching. Although neither had been consulted in at least five years, past experience with them had provided many insights and we hoped that theirs would be another important lens through which to understand this post-220 world.

The first tarot card reading was a simple four-card spread corresponding to the four conditions What Is At Hand, Past Influences, Ponder This, and What To Do. While we found significant meaning from each of the first three cards, the fourth card, corresponding to "What To Do," provided the most important counsel of all: "Things are out of balance. Practice patience and perseverance." "Patience and Perseverance" became our second most favorite mantra.

Next up was the I Ching. For this reading, we focused our thoughts on Maia and where she was/how she was now. Following the I Ching instructions we took three coins, assigned a numerical value to getting either heads or tails, and tossed them together six separate times. The total value of each toss was represented by either a solid line or a divided line, with each drawn above the other. The final configuration of six lines corresponded to one of sixty-four hexagrams whose characteristics and significance were fully described in the I Ching.

This is a brief summary of what resulted when we asked the I Ching, "Tell us about Maia Felisse":

Hexagram 55: Feng – Abundance (clarity within, movement without)

The Judgment:
Abundance has success.
The king attains abundance.
Be not sad. Be like the sun at midday.

The Commentary:
There is only one means to making foundations firm in times of greatness, namely, spiritual expansion… Abundance can endure only if ever larger groups are brought to share in it, for only then can the movement continue without turning into its opposite. One should give light to the whole world.

The image revealed was so very positive and powerful, and fit well with the other signs we had experienced indicating that Maia, wherever/however she might be, was in a good place. Additionally, we were provided with what was to become our third favorite mantra: "Be not sad. Be like the sun at midday."

In this way we began the first morning of our four-day Truro retreat. The remaining days, filled with walks along the coastal cliffs and empty beaches, candle lightings and incense, tears and laughter, provided just the right atmosphere for us to continue trying to find meaning and direction in this post-220 journey. Although we often joked that these crazy amazing signs, dreams, and synchronicities could either be the beginning of enlightenment or the beginning of insanity, we knew we were not going insane.

The last journal entry for April described the sighting of a very unusual cloud formation.

Lori: "Late in the day on April 22, I put together a special 21st birthday present for Felicia, one of Maia's best friends from childhood. The gift included a bottle of Lucky Star wine and a shot glass Maia had brought back from Jamaica a few years ago. Although I knew Felicia was out to dinner with her family, I had a few errands to do and decided to drop the gifts off at her house anyway. A little while later, as I was heading north on the highway, I noticed a very dramatic cloud formation ahead in the distance. As I drove closer, I couldn't believe my eyes: the cloud looked just like a dragon's head with fire and smoke coming out of its mouth. There were absolutely no other clouds in the sky, making this particular formation even more noticeable. It remained directly in front of me for a mile or two until the roadway turned and I lost sight of it. When I got to the mall and parked the car, I noticed that someone had sent me a multimedia text message. It was from Felicia: a photograph of a Chinese restaurant placemat that zoomed in on the Year of the Dragon (Maia's year), accompanied by, of course, a fire breathing dragon. Another amazing coincidence that still makes me smile whenever I remember it."

May

May began with three wonderful dreams occurring on the same day: Lori dreamt she and Brian were walking through an archway with a giant blue jay perched on top. Brian had a dream in which he and Lori were on a beautiful tropical island paradise, first alone, then surrounded by lots of people, then alone again. And Brian's mother, Virginia, recounted the following dream in an email later that same day:

"Maia was the focal point and I was gathering flowers. The amazing part is that Maia's outfit and the hundreds of flowers that I had gathered for her were all the exact shade of rosy pink. She asked me why all the flowers were the same color and I answered that they matched her outfit which was a t-shirt and shorts. The flowers were everywhere and kept multiplying until we could hardly move and all in the same exact color. She was puzzled (with that questioning look that she used) and we both laughed. It was a fun dream and I awoke with a very peaceful feeling. I believe it was a visit from Maia and I hope she comes back often."

The month of May also included some very important events: the 14th anniversary of Lori's mother's death, Sean's graduation from college, and our first Mother's Day without Maia.

Lori: "Thinking about celebrating Sean's graduation and Mother's Day without Maia was too much to bear so I arranged with my colleagues to leave work early on Thursday, the day before Sean's graduation and the anniversary of my mother's death. As I hurried to get away, I could feel tears brimming in my eyes. I made it to my car, started the engine, and then totally lost it as the car's clock, which was set a few minutes fast, flashed 11:11, Maia's time! I drove the four blocks home, tears streaming down my face, feeling completely overcome by sadness. When I got home, I headed straight to the kitchen for a glass of water. Incredibly, the microwave clock also read 11:11! ... 'Yes, yes, I know you're still with me,' I wailed, 'but this is so hard and I don't know what to do.'

I went into the 'Maia Room' (where we had created a fireplace shrine with the urn that contained her ashes, photos, candles, and numerous mementos) and lit some incense. Then it hit me – we would not be here for Mother's Day. I started to feel terrible, like I was abandoning

Maia on such an important day. As a compromise, I gathered photos of Maia's grandmothers and great grandmothers (all of whom were deceased but one) and placed them on the fireplace mantle. I lit a candle and quietly prayed for them to take good care of our Maia. It was the strangest thing but it truly brought me comfort to imagine her surrounded by the spirit and energy of these wonderful women."

Sean's graduation and the party afterward with his roommates and their families were bittersweet, but we did our best to shower him with happiness and celebrate this important milestone. Excusing ourselves a little early, we left for Truro and another weekend retreat. We spent a lot of time outdoors in the beautiful weather but we also made time to read, try another tarot card spread, and work with our set of runes for the first time.

Not surprisingly, a few meaningful coincidences occurred: 1) Lori notices that the book she is reading, Many Lives, Many Masters, was first published the year Maia was born (1988) and that this particular book is the 20th anniversary edition; and 2) Brian picks the rune "Ansuz" as he asks the question, "What am I to make of all that has been happening?" Because Ansuz is the messenger, the rune of prophecy and revelation, we interpret its significance to mean: "receive the messages; take time to receive what the universe has to offer."

On May 14th, we both took the day off from work to make our last trip to Amherst. Not wanting to bring everything back with us to Clinton, we found a local emergency relief center to accept most of Maia's clothing, left a few things for her roommates or other UMass friends, and packed up the car with the rest of her belongings. As we drove home, we listened to a CD of country music tunes that one of Maia's friends had created for us in recognition of her love for country music. The collection of songs brought equal amounts of tears, smiles, and head-shaking, but truly made the final hours of this very difficult day easier to bear.

Four other significant events helped bring the month of May to a close:

May 20th: the third month anniversary of Maia's passing and the installation and dedication of the Maia Felisse McDermott memorial plaque at Congregation Shaarei Zedeck in Clinton. A few prayers, some lovely music, and a small gathering of friends back at the house afterward.

May 21st: The school district Brian worked for had a big event to celebrate the approval of a new middle/high school, an achievement of great local importance and one which would probably not have occurred without Brian's tireless leadership, made even more impressive by how he kept forging ahead despite the personal pain of Maia's passing. Local dignitaries, special guests, and the entire student body gathered in the school gym for the ceremony. In addition, one lone hummingbird had somehow found its way inside. Symbolizing the accomplishment of that which appears impossible, inimitable endurance, and the miracle of joyful living, this littlest of guests hovered above the rafters throughout the entire program.

May 22nd: Brian dreamed about six wolves, one of which was really large and white, and two polar bears approaching him and a group of other people. Fearing the wolves would harm them, Brian threw a large rock to ward them off. One wolf effortlessly caught the rock in its mouth, gently put it on the ground, but did not come any closer. Upon awaking, Brian reflected upon the possible meaning of the dream and noted that there was no indication from the wolves that they meant to hurt anyone.

"When wolf shows up, it is time to breathe new life into your life rituals. Find a new path, take a new journey, take control of your life. You are the governor of your life." (Animal-Speak, pgs. 323-325)

In light of his increasingly arduous and frustrating work environment, "I am the governor of my life" instantly became one of his most important mantras.

May 25th: Lori notices another coincidence. While reviewing an old journal in which she kept track of her Motherpeace tarot reading experiences, she sees that the last entry is dated 9/18/2005 at **2:20** p.m. Reading further, she sees that the "Outcome" card is the Crone, the same card that turned up in the most recent tarot spread corresponding to the "Near Future" position. Was there a connection?

Lori: "According to Motherpeace, the Crone is a symbol for turning within to the source of wisdom and lighting the way for others, a power I would welcome into my life without hesitation and with great honor."

June

June's arrival brought forth a huge sigh of relief. The lengthening days and warmer temperatures, flowers and trees in full bloom, and the end of the school year were exactly what we needed. We had just been through the most difficult, painful, and paradoxically enlightening 100 days of our lives, and were more than ready to take a break from the stress of work and embrace the natural world as it entered its most glorious season, summer.

We still felt like emotional pendulums when it came to thinking about Maia. Sometimes upbeat, remembering how much love and energy she brought into our lives and the lives of countless others, and somewhat consoled by knowing she no longer had to endure the inevitable struggles and anguish of human life. But oftentimes we were still depressed, saddened, and overcome with despair knowing that she was gone from this life and we would forever miss her hugs, kisses, and serendipitous adventures. We knew our feelings were understandable and everyone advised us to be gentle and accepting of ourselves, and to take whatever time we needed to heal and regain balance.

Fortunately, we continued to receive support from our dear community of family and friends, and from many of Maia's friends who would reach out to us with offers of companionship, stories of Maia, and appreciation for her "carpe diem" example. These contributed enormously to our ability to recover from the shock of Maia's death. But perhaps of even greater importance were our own ongoing efforts to be more receptive to the signs and synchronicities by which we felt Maia's spiritual presence most strongly. We still didn't know how it happened (i.e., the meaningful dreams, signs, and synchronicities) but we could not deny their reality and kept on looking for explanations that made sense.

Like the astonishing gathering of blue jays in our tree, two major happenings in June will forever represent indisputable evidence for the reality of "life after life" and Loni's "porous veil" metaphor.

Lori: "In the early evening of June 11th, I found myself slipping into the all too familiar Friday depression and headed to bed. Even though Sean was coming home and we had plans to join some friends for dinner, I just couldn't muster the energy to get up. Eventually I fell asleep and awoke to Sean's voice outside in our driveway. I looked at the clock and saw that it was 2:20 a.m. I fell back asleep and just before waking had an extremely vivid dream.

In the dream, Maia was about 21, dressed as she often was in jeans and a sweatshirt, keys hanging loosely in her hand. 'Hey, Mom, how ya doing?' she asked, 'I need $2,000.' I remember getting upset and started to say, 'Uh oh, what happened, what did you do now?' but I woke up before I could learn why she needed the money. I immediately told Brian about the dream and remembered feeling terrible for automatically assuming that she was in some type of trouble.

Later that morning over breakfast with Sean, we started to talk about the summer and any travel plans we might have. 'How about going to Ireland?' Sean proposed. I looked at him, 'Yeah, right,' I said. 'No really, I'm serious,' he replied. 'Really?' I asked, 'How's that gonna happen?' 'I'm going to send you and dad for your 25th anniversary,' he answered. 'You can't afford that,' I started to say, and then remembered the dream with Maia asking for $2,000 – was there a connection?

Over the next few minutes, Sean did some more explaining. Apparently he and Maia, prompted by my sister, had talked about doing something for our anniversary but then she died before anything definite could be planned. So on his own, Sean did some research about traveling abroad, identified a bona fide tour package, and contacted a few family members to request financial assistance. Although he indicated that he was still working on acquiring money for the airfare, he was confident that he would have enough to send us to Ireland.

Still not convinced that he could afford this trip, I told him about my dream and said, 'Tell you what, Sean, we'll 'give' Maia the $2,000 and she can use it to help send us to Ireland.'

P.S. Amazingly, our plane tickets came to $954.40 each - just under $2,000!"

The second major happening occurred on Father's Day weekend. As with Mother's Day, celebrating without a flesh and blood Maia was going to be tough so, with Sean's OK, we made some plans to get away to New Hampshire for some hiking and live music. One of Brian's favorite singer/songwriters was performing in the little town of Bethlehem, right up the road from the White Mountains' Falling Waters Trail. This sounded practically ideal so Lori bought tickets, arranged accommodations, identified potential restaurants, and found a few other things to do.

Similar to Mother's Day, we felt bad about leaving Maia on Father's Day so we gathered all the grandfather and great grandfather photos we had and placed them next to the grandmother photos on the fireplace mantel. As before, it gave us a great sense of peace and comfort imagining the loving spirits of these exceptional men (all deceased except one) surrounding her.

Lori: "We left early Saturday morning, drove straight to the Falling Waters Trail, and spent the day hiking. Afterward we checked into our hotel in Littleton, NH, showered and dressed, and had some extra time to decide where to go for dinner. Even though I had already scoped out some possibilities in the area, Brian took out his cell phone and searched for restaurants anyway. 'I don't believe it,' he exclaimed, 'we definitely have to check out this restaurant!' 'What restaurant?' I asked. 'The Maia Papaya Café!'

I couldn't believe it either. For one thing, we had never heard of a restaurant with Maia's name in it. But more importantly, nothing about it had shown up for me during my internet restaurant searches, only for Brian."

As fate would have it, the Maia Papaya Café was only open for breakfast and lunch, which meant we would have to wait until the following day. That day, of course, was Father's Day. To top it off, as we were taking a photo of Brian in front of the restaurant's sign, he noticed that if you cut off the 'ya' in 'Papaya', you get 'Papa' which is what Maia and Sean called him when they were little, and, subsequently, 'Maia Papa.' Without a doubt, this was the most wonderful Father's Day surprise ever.

Father's Day at the Maia Papaya Café (Bethlehem, NH).

One more interesting note: After breakfast we decided to drive to Mt. Washington and check out the surrounding area. On our way there, just a mile or two down the road from the Maia Papaya, we noticed a couple of cars stopped on the side of the road – a moose! We pulled over as well, and spent about five minutes in an eye-to-eye gaze with this most noble animal. Eventually we had to drive off, but it kept a solid gaze with Lori until we were out of sight.

Here is an excerpt from Ted Andrews about the Moose:

*"Keynote: Primal Feminine Energies and the Magic of Life and Death … (The moose) has a unique ability to plunge to the bottom of lakes, and remain there feeding for up to a full minute before surfacing in a burst with fresh greens dangling from their mouths … It reflects the ability of the individual to learn to go back into the depths and draw new life and nourishment from it. The moose can teach the ability to move from the outer world to the inner. It can teach how to cross from life to death and back to stronger life. It teaches how to use the thin thread that separates life and death to one's advantage." (*Animal-Speak*, pg. 287)*

It was becoming pretty apparent to us that there is tremendous mystery and power just beyond our fingertips, but ever so close as to occasionally give us glimpses, and somehow our Maia was most definitely involved. We still didn't completely understand and perhaps we never would, but as we began sharing our post-220 experiences with others, a journey we were affectionately starting to call "Maia's Magical Mystical Journey," we received back a few encouraging thoughts and stories, letting us know we were not alone:

From cc: "Moments like the Maia Papaya give me hope and wonder. That is so cool how those things happen. She is definitely here."

From Devon: "This afternoon I was getting ready to go to a youth group thing at church. I opened my box where I keep earrings and tried to find a matching pair of posts, (I either lose one or one breaks most of the time leaving me with mismatched pairs). I decided since I was in a hurry I would just go with whatever two colors I picked out of the box first. I bet you know what they were ... pink and yellow :) Love you guys, see you soon."

From JoJo: "Thinking about Maia ... I remember being aware of my father's essence close to me ... quite a few times in my youth. I could FEEL his selfness near to me ... different than thinking about him. Is it the same with Maia? I know she communicates by bringing you two and things together ... like the Maia Papaya ... and other wondrous things. Life does hold such beauty ... and I am beginning to think that death may hold breathtaking beauty. There is so much that I wish I understood better."

July

July began with an interesting phone call from Brian's uncle Robert, a follow-up to a brief visit we had with him and his wife Ellen just a few days before. During that visit, we had spoken honestly about the feelings and experiences we were having in response to Maia's death. We described some of the synchronicities, signs, and dreams, and the paradoxical position we were in: still very, very sad yet feeling awestruck and strangely blessed at the same time.

We also shared with them some lingering concerns we had about attending an upcoming McDermott family reunion, which was planned for July 10 in Chappaqua, NY. Maia had been with us last summer when we went and not having her with us this year, we knew, would be tough. Robert and Ellen agreed that we must do what we felt was right for us, and reminded us that everyone in the family was thinking of Maia and us with nothing but love and encouragement.

Robert's follow-up phone call was to tell us about a conversation he had just had with his brother Joe, who wanted to know how we were doing. "Oh they are managing as best they can and feeling Maia's presence through occasional signs and synchronicities which they are trying to understand," Robert told him. Joe, who was not ordinarily inclined toward the mystical, didn't quite know how to respond and their conversation ended soon after. Within a few minutes of hanging up, Joe called Robert back. "Hey, you know those synchronicities you were talking about?" he began, "Well I was just reaching into a cabinet for something and thinking about our conversation, and you won't believe it … I pulled out a package of 'Carpe Diem' coffee. Didn't even know I had it!" Yep, that would be a synchronicity.

A few days later, Brian's niece, Julia, and her fiancé, George, who we hadn't seen since the Memorial Service, came to Clinton for a short visit. It was very nice to spend time with them but it was also tough because Maia would have been one of Julia's bridesmaids and any talk about the upcoming November wedding brought forth a mix of emotions.

Early the next morning, the beginning of the 20th week since Maia's car crash, Lori experienced the following dream:

Lori: "I was sitting at a picnic table with Brian, Sean, Julia, and George. Off in the distance was a tree filled with thousands of beautiful butterflies. Parading under and around the tree were lots of little people (fairies and elves maybe) and hundreds more butterflies. As I turned my focus back to Brian and the others, I noticed two gigantic, iridescent blue butterflies holding onto the table's umbrella pole and waving the tips of their beautiful wings at me. It was such a charming dream and, since butterflies often represent spiritual transformation and life after death, I think this was Maia's way of telling me, 'Stop worrying, Mom, I'm doing just fine'."

The 20th week ended with a few very intriguing events, the most enigmatic of which was the mysterious appearance of Maia's peridot ring that she had received many years ago from Brian's mother. Lori had been looking for this ring since February and had begun to think that maybe Maia was wearing it the night she crashed. What makes this a "mysterious appearance" is where the ring was found: in a little white box on top of a pile of photos on Maia's dresser. Not only was the location in plain view, but Lori had been the one to put the pile of photos there in the first place and can vouch that there was no little white box anywhere near those photos. When it became clear that neither one of us had placed the box on the photos, we both realized that it truly was a "mysterious" appearance.

A second event occurred on our way to the McDermott reunion in New York. After picking up Sean in Boston, we headed west on the Massachusetts Turnpike toward New York. Despite the fact that we would be seeing lots of loving family members, both of us had pretty heavy hearts. We really missed Maia and last year's memories of her at the reunion actually increased our sad feelings. Just then we notice a large coach bus with an unfamiliar name and logo ahead of us. As we got closer, we could see that it was a "Lucky Star" bus and that its logo is comprised of the constellation Pleiades and a cute little dragon offering up a peace sign. Immediately we began to smile because two of the symbols we associate with Maia, dragons (because she was born during the Chinese Year of the Dragon) and stars (because "Maia" is the name of one of the stars in the Pleiades cluster), were both on this one bus.

The third event to cap off the end of the 20th week came in the form of a framed photograph given to us by our brother-in-law, Tom. The photo, of an airplane wing as seen from inside the plane's cabin, was taken by Tom in February. Just above the wing, appearing to be very far out in the distance, is a tiny, hard to see, small bright spot. Here is part of what Tom wrote about this photo:

"When we left Clinton [after the Memorial Service], Michele & Devon went to New York, Damon back to Denver. I flew home alone on a half empty plane, sitting by myself and gazing out the window, thinking of Maia, you all and Sean, and all that had come to pass in the preceding days. As we ascended through the weather over Boston, I kept watching the sky, thinking of Maia, and took some pictures as the plane emerged from the fog. When I got home and developed the film, I saw the photographs and thought this one reminded me of Maia, of her freedom, of her presence, of her everywhereness. I made the prints just this week, and after they were dry I looked at them more carefully and noticed a small bright spot in the photo. I thought about it for a while and I remembered what Devon had said at the service about Maia and the snow in Austin. And I know that you can get artifacts when printing photographs. But I just think it's Maia helping me make this for you. It's the twinkle in her eye. It's Maia's star."

On July 18th we began our extraordinary Ireland Anniversary Adventure, twelve days of travel made possible by the amazing Sean and, in a most profound way, Maia. As if to emphasize this point, Lori noticed another dragon cloud formation outside our airplane just after take off.

We spent our first night in Dublin. Waking up early the next morning, Lori recounted a dream in which a woman was being interviewed about the death of her 5-year-old child and telling the interviewer, "It's not really all that bad." Lori woke up before learning what the woman meant.

Right after breakfast we picked up our rental car and headed west toward Killarney. Although the car came equipped with a CD player, we hadn't thought to bring any CDs, so Lori tried to find a good station on the radio. Rather unexpectedly, she came across what sounded like a country music station, Maia's favorite kind of music. The song playing at the time, "Ride On" by Christy Moore, had a beautiful melody and a very timely chorus: *"Ride on, see you, I could never go with you, no matter how I wanted to."* As the song ended, we drove out of reception range and never did manage to find that station again.

Later that night, we did some internet searching and found the complete lyrics as well as the following analysis of "Ride On" by the composer himself, Jimmy McCarthy:

"… *purely and simply, it is a song of parting. The parting of lovers, the parting of emigrants from their homeland and friends, the parting when illness or accident takes the life of a loved one … Life is hard. Ride On."* (www.mudcat.org)

Throughout the following 10 days, both Maia and Sean were never far from our thoughts, and we never took for granted even a second of this most amazing trip.

One day after we returned, and the day before our 25th wedding anniversary, Lori made the following journal entry:

Death is not the end for you.
In our thoughts, dreams, actions,
and deepest inner soul, you live on.
Life has never felt more profound
yet your smile reminds me "Lighten up!"
Don't think, just do.
Patience & perseverance.
I will love you forever.

August

August started off with Brian's reluctant return to work after a five-week leave of absence. Almost as if to emphasize the hardship his job as Superintendent had become, he woke up the next day at 2:20 a.m. after having a dream about his turtle tattoo (an exact replica of the one Maia had) bleeding through his shirt.

Lori experienced a much more positive post-vacation re-entry since her summer work hours had been reduced to two days per week. Her week ended with a wonderful day of canoeing with her friend Laurie, the highlight of which was being "escorted" by an eagle who crisscrossed the river four or five times, always just a little ahead of them as they headed back to the canoe drop-in point. In addition, later that evening Lori received the following email from her sister Meri:

"Just a note to let you know I've passed the 100 mark on my pledge to do that many mitzvoth in Maia's memory so that her name should be for a blessing. It is comforting that I can share this with you on the 36th anniversary of the passing of our father, Robert Berger. Just like a song we sing, one mitzvah leads to another! My next goal is to complete 180 by February 20th, as the number '18' - and all of its place-holding zeroes - represents the value of the word Chai ... 'life'."

What a comfort to know that Maia's life and "after life" were still having a most positive impact on so many lives ...

One week later on August 14th Brian woke up and recounted the following dream: "I finally saw Maia in a dream. She was wearing a blue flowery dress. She turned to me. We gave each other an 'I love you' hug. I kissed her on her cheek. She seemed happy."

When he was finished, Lori described an interesting dream she had just had: "I dreamed that you and I were on, or getting ready to go on, 'a higher path.' No one, no thing was around us. I turned to you and said, 'We're on a higher path together'."

As the last word left Lori's lips, we heard the sound of a blue jay. Brian looked out the window and saw one at the bird feeder. Minutes later we heard more squawking so Lori looked out and saw not one but two blue jays in the tree outside our bedroom. Two very special dreams and one quite astounding synchronicity - the impact of which remained for many months as the two jays stayed with us through the beginning of winter.

Not too long after this dream/synchronicity sequence, Lori posted a "Maya the Bee" video clip on Facebook so people would know how Maia got her nickname "the Bee." As a result, another interesting coincidence, which we learned about from Lori's niece Kirston, occurred:

"The day after I saw the 'Maya the Bee' video on Facebook and learned about its connection to Maia for the first time, my boyfriend, Gary, woke up singing the chorus, 'Maya, Maya the Bee.' Strange thing is, he had not seen the video clip and had never heard the song before!"

August's most important event was to arrive on the 31st, Maia's 22nd birthday. After much thought, we sent the following letter to our family and friends:

Dear Family & Friends,

As many of you know, Maia was born on August 31st, a little over a week from today. And as many of you might imagine, we've been wondering, "What are we going to do?" Without Maia here in the flesh & blood, her birthday, we know, might be a very difficult day for us and for countless others who know and love and miss her still.

So, after thinking through lots of possibilities, we finally decided that what we need most (and what we believe Maia would want) is to bring people together and have a good time: eat, drink, make music, dance in the rain, and celebrate our beloved Maia. So, if you're free, please plan to join us: Saturday, August 28, 2010 (7:00 p.m. - ?) - here at our home. Come when you want, stay as long as you can .... (Those who can't come we know will be with us in spirit.)

"Let's celebrate her life from night til morning."
From "Maia's Song" by Giddens Rateau

Approximately 60 people gathered to celebrate Maia's life, and while there were some tears, there was more often than not laughter, music, happy memories, and stories of how Maia's presence is still felt by so many of her friends. With an outdoor fire burning, a few hardy souls stayed until late into the night. Lori went to bed around 4, but Brian managed to greet the first light of dawn, literally celebrating Maia's life from night til morning.

Later that day we were remembering the days preceding Maia's birth, which was almost two weeks past her official due date, and quite unexpectedly made a new discovery. The first time the two of us met was in an evening graduate class at Texas A&M University on Aug. 30, 1982. The very next day, Aug. 31st, we had our first ever conversation. Exactly six years later, Lori's labor with Maia began on the 30th and she was born at 3:08 a.m. on the 31st. Another interesting coincidence or something more? We may never know. But there is no doubt that we will forevermore celebrate the magic of our first meeting and Maia's birth together.

On Maia's birthday, the 31st, Lori took the day off and Brian left work as soon as he could, around 10 a.m. We wanted to spend this day alone together but had made plans for a very unusual appointment.

With all of the books we had been reading, conversations we'd been having, and mystical experiences we were encountering, we were convinced that a spiritual world existed, and that Maia lived on in some form. We wanted so much to strengthen our connection with her and increase our understanding of how this could all even be possible, and so we made an appointment with an ordained "Pan-denominational Metaphysical Minister' from the south shore, a.k.a. a spiritual medium. We were not sure what to expect but were willing to give it a try.

When we arrived for our 2:00 appointment, we were greeted by the very cheerful and easy going Reverend Shari. Since this was our first time with a medium, she began by giving us an overview of how metaphysics correlates with what we know through science.

Shari: "Everything is vibration, energy. We are denser (slower, lower) than your daughter is now. When I'm communicating with Spirit, I pay more attention to visions. I can 'feel' how they passed, or 'hear' like I hear my own thoughts or sometimes with my outer ears (clairaudience). I sense through vibrational frequencies – image, sounds, feelings. We are energy – just denser. Not sure exactly how this communication happens, just that it does."

After about 20 more minutes of overview type information, Shari began to communicate various messages/conversations with spiritual beings whose characteristics correlated amazingly well with Maia, Lori's mother, father, and grandfather, and Brian's grandfather and late brother-in-law. In addition, there were certain pieces of information exchanged that Shari had absolutely no way of knowing thereby totally convincing us of her authenticity.

The actual "reading" lasted an hour but we were with her for almost two. Following are some of the most important messages we received from Maia:

"I am fine, don't worry. It's all OK up here. I was being stupid."

"Papa, you took good care of me. Be patient. Don't give up hope on yourself ... I'm sorry for the problems I caused you. It was not what I meant to do."

Shari: "Did you do something different to your house recently ... to the outside?" (We indicate yes, about $10,000 worth of fencing and new landscaping.) "She likes it."

Shari: "I sense an honest sense of humor about her ... she's saying something like *'The things that motivate me can be an ass kicker'.*"

Shari: "Does she have a friend who's blaming herself for the accident? Maia wants you to tell her *'Cut the shit. I will not be responsible for someone feeling guilty over this'.*"

Shari: "I'm sensing from Maia that there's a calmness, acceptance to the whole thing. She's saying 'like there's divinity in it.' It's a happening that set off other, good, happenings. She's at peace with it. .... She's giving me an image of John Walsh, you know who that is? The man who started the TV show 'America's Most Wanted' after his own son was murdered. She's telling you, *'There are two ways to go with it'.*"

Shari: "She's actually making fun of you two being here. Such a sense of humor. Now she's putting up a crystal ball and going 'woo woo' ... really making fun of you."

Shari (from Maia to Lori): *"Thank you for giving/allowing me my freedom. I understand how hard it was for you. We acted like we were both so different but we were really the same. Sometimes we put assumptions/ projections of fear on ourselves by others; we both did that to each other. It's OK. We'd laugh our asses off if we realized that. ... Don't beat yourself up. It's all good. Sometimes it takes two."*

Shari: "She's definitely Daddy's girl ...(from Maia to Brian): *'You were easy to mold.'* Mom was a little wiser... Now she's asking about having her ring ... do you have it?"

Shari (from Maia to Sean): *"Don't try to be too strong. Don't stop your feelings. Get it out in the way you know how. I love you."*

Brian asks "How are you?"

Shari (from Maia): *"I'm just fine. The glass is half full, daddy."*

Shari: "She wants you to keep celebrating her joy, her time. She's still living."

After our session, which was indeed life-changing, we headed to the coast to have dinner. Our heads were spinning from what we had just experienced and we knew we would need lots of time to make sense of it all. Most immediately, however, was a huge feeling of love for Maia, a newly awakened appreciation for life's mysterious ways, and a recognition that this post-220 journey would be unlike anything we could have ever imagined.

September

The past six months had been a roller coaster of emotions, self-reflection, spiritual seeking, and dealing with the hard face of reality. Yet because of all the special remembrances of Maia from family and friends, the realization that she lived more in her 21 years than most of us live in 50, and the undeniable evidence of her continued presence in our lives, we were, relatively-speaking, feeling OK. As Lori stated in a posting on Maia's Facebook page: "Peace of mind is slowly emerging from the earthquake that was your death. We can see the glass half full."

Reluctantly resigning ourselves to the fact of no more flesh and blood Maia, we became more intent on preserving her legacy of compassion, adventure, and sparkling presence, and focusing on becoming more open to her spiritually. Admittedly, some of this did seem pretty unbelievable but we were committed to delving deep into alternative ways to understand life, death, and life beyond life.

Unfortunately, "understanding life, death, and life beyond life" is not rocket science, i.e., it is not something with infallibly objective truths and calculations. As Rev. Shari reminded us: *There are some things that we just can't understand with our minds and just have to trust with our souls and hearts … Remember stronger and more powerful than any reasonings of the mind are the 'knowings' of the soul.*

Nevertheless, we had a huge desire to understand whatever we could about what, why, and how things were happening, and fortunately we knew we were not really alone. There were many other people exploring similarly and lots of great resources, and as Brian often said, "Maia is so our teacher," the greatest resource of all.

9/22: Autumn Equinox and Full Moon - We made a return visit to the sacred grove on Karen and Paul's land. Karen lit candles and incense while Brian placed his hand engraved "Maia's Gap" stone in the rock wall opening which we caused by our taking large stones to make the Spring Equinox fire pit. Paul had named this space "Maia's Gap" in light-hearted reference to the large gap Maia had between her two front teeth.

Later that night, Karen posted the following on Facebook:

"A toast to Maia, to the equinox tonight, to the light of the full moon breaking the clouds, to humor and love carrying the day, the night, and us all, all the way through!"

9/25: The last Saturday in September found us heading west to Sturbridge, MA for the Natural Living Expo, a very large holistic health event. In addition to workshops and exhibits on natural foods, massage, fitness, etc., there were many related to more spiritual and esoteric matters as well.

We attended three different workshops and enjoyed walking around the main exhibit hall with hundreds of other people interested in the same things as we were. It was a relief to see things like tarot card readings, spiritual mediums, aura analysis, and dream interpretation "out of the closet" and becoming more main stream.

The day ended with two very significant coincidences. During a workshop entitled "Meet Your Guardian Angel" those present (about 150 of us) were lead through a brief meditation that would supposedly help us connect with our own guardian angel beings. To prove that this was real, we were told to ask for something that would manifest within 24 hours. Although neither of us had really "felt" any type of angelic presence, both of us made a request.

Lori: "When our last event ended, I had a really strong urge to just get on the road and head home. We were probably on the Massachusetts Turnpike no more than ten minutes when I noticed a large coach bus up ahead. As we got closer, I could tell that it was a 'Lucky Star' bus. Passing along side, I could see the familiar Pleiades constellation and dorky little dragon making a peace sign. Suddenly I started to laugh out loud and then immediately broke down in tears. When I calmed myself enough, I explained to Brian: 'At the angel workshop we went to, I asked my guardian angel, if it truly existed, to let me see Maia. But this is not what I meant!'"

After we arrived home, Brian headed straight to the Maia room and brought Lori a photo of Maia taken at a Red Sox game a few years ago: baseball cap to the side, goofy grin on her face, and hands flashing us a peace sign. The connection was so obvious and we found ourselves again smiling and amazed by the wonder of it all.

October

Autumn was upon us. Though the days were still warm, the dark of night began to arrive earlier and earlier. Fortunately, the month was filled with many Maiaspirit moments, intriguing, heartwarming, and at times, quite humorous.

First to unfold was the wonderful coincidence that occurred during Julia's Bridal Shower in San Antonio. As a shower present, Lori thought it would be nice to make candle holders from stained glass, a craft she had learned six years ago. As an extra special touch, she decided to use some colored glass Maia had given her as a Christmas-Chanukah present the previous December. At the time, Maia had said, *"I have no clue what you're going to do with this."* No doubt she would totally approve of creating candle cubes for her cousin Julia and George.

Stained glass candle holders for Julia and George.

In response to an email from Brian to his sister Marise (Julia's mother) asking how the shower went, Marise sent this note:

"Not only did the Shower go well for Julia, but it was so so special because of your gifts. When Julia opened the gift made by Lori with Maia's choice of glass, we could not believe it…They are so beautiful. But a side note is that Julia and I looked for weeks for two candle holders for the bride and groom table and could

not find any that were right. I said to Julia the day before the shower, 'We'll know them when we see them.' When Julia opened the packages, we gasped. Julia said, 'Here they are.'... Maia was so present in the room at that moment."

A few days later, Marise and her husband Hollis, formally announced the establishment of the Maia Felisse McDermott Memorial Scholarship at UMass-Amherst. The scholarship would target students in the Bachelor's Degree with Individual Concentration program, which was where Maia was able to create her own major in broadcast journalism. In their announcement, Marise and Hollis wrote:

"In celebration of Maia's life, the Maia Felisse McDermott Memorial Scholarship is being established at UMass Amherst to help, encourage, and inspire us to 'Seize the Day.' We invite you to join us in creating this special tribute to her."

To us, this was a most meaningful way to ensure that Maia's spirit would continue to shine upon her UMass community.

10/17: Lori had lunch with Nancy, a parent of one of Maia's best friends at UMass. They talked a lot about Maia, her friendship with Nancy's daughter, the impact of her death, and her continuing presence in so many people's lives. In addition, Nancy gave Lori a very special present – a dress covered with pink & white roses. The dress had been hanging in Nancy's closet for the past three years but just this morning had fallen off its hanger - all by itself. Nancy felt strongly that this was a message from Maia.

October ended with three very memorable events. The first was attending a large group session with Rev. Rita Berkowitz, spiritual medium and co-author of the book <u>The Complete Idiot's Guide to Communicating with Spirits</u>. Her program was filled with humor, explanations about why and how she is able to receive images/messages from spiritual beings, and convincing demonstrations that had profound connections to some of the people in the audience. It was a pretty amazing evening and encouraging to be around others who shared many of the same views and experiences we had.

The next morning Lori woke up and told Brian about a very unusual dream she had just had with Henry, a little pug belonging to one of Maia's best friends from Clinton. In the dream, Henry was running around, jumping into her arms, chasing other dogs, and then at the end of the dream, he was running around with a dripping white paintbrush in his mouth.

What was really unusual was the vividness of this dream. Lori described actually "feeling" Henry in her arms, his puppyish body squirming around and the solidity of his little chest and legs. In fact, it sounded very much like how Rev. Berkowitz described some of her experiences with spirits coming through her, that she could "feel" their body types, their stoutness or frailty, their hunched shoulders or strong, upright postures. "I think this 'feeling' I had with Henry may be sort of what she was describing to us."

Later that day, Lori was raking leaves and had a sudden impulse to rake right up next to the house near the water faucet and hose. "Yo, Brian," she yelled, "you'll never believe this one." Lo and behold, buried deep under the leaves, was an old paintbrush with, you guessed it, drips of white paint.

During the late afternoon, with the sun hanging low in the sky, both of us paused to admire the tenacity and loveliness of the last bloom on the "Beauty Within" rose bush, given to us in honor of Maia. Speaking aloud to no one in particular, Brian said, "The rose is still blooming." Echoing his thought in her mind, Lori mused silently, "The <u>yellow</u> rose is still blooming." Just at that very moment, a blue jay flew straight in front of that very lovely yellow rose.

"Beauty Within" Rose

November

In addition to Thanksgiving, two very important family events were coming up in November: a reunion with Lori's siblings in North Carolina to celebrate her oldest brother's 60th birthday, and the wedding of Julia and George in San Antonio.

To prepare ourselves and others, we decided to communicate something about what we had been experiencing these past eight months, in particular, that while we were still feeling the pain of Maia's death, we were also on a very hopeful path of recovery and renewal. Most of all, we did not want anyone to worry about us and detract from the celebration of these two momentous occasions.

After a lot of thinking and discussion, we came up with the following poem which we eventually sent to many relatives and even some of our close friends:

220

a knock at the door
let in the ripple
that flooded our lives
with the shock of your
death
friends and family
philosophers and mystics
deacons and cantors and devout followers
of all faiths and no faiths
surrounded us with love
guided
supported
nourished us
20 blue jays gathered in our tree
squawking emissaries between earth and sky
"death is not the end"
is what we think they said
but there is no doubt
they were there
for you
memories and dreams
coincidence that matters
signs that call out
make our heads shake and our lips smile
ancient ways and modern modes
coax us slowly beyond grief and sadness
transforming our lives
into what? we know not
yet with patience and perseverance
we try every day
to be not sad
to be like the sun at midday
living life as you would
compassion and carpe diem
we honor your memory
celebrate your spirit
knowing and hoping
you are with us
always.

In response to receiving "220" one of our friends sent us the following email: *"There are blue jays residing in the tree outside my window. They will remind me of Maia until they depart for the winter. They return every spring and will remind me anew."*

The first big event, Mitch's 60th birthday celebration, brought all three of Lori's siblings, her brother-in-law Bill, and Brian to Myrtle Beach. Lovely warm weather, Frisbee, wiffle ball, and walks on the beach, a little golf (of course), and a few Maiaspirit moments to make us laugh, reflect, and wonder.

Although Lori headed out on Tuesday (11/9) to drive down by car with Mitch, Brian was planning to take a plane directly to Myrtle Beach on Thursday, which happened to be 11/11.

Brian: "Since I had an 8:00 a.m. flight on Thursday, I spent all of Wednesday night getting ready. Sometime after 2 a.m. I was drawn outside to look for Pleiades. I walked out and gazed up. The starlit sky was amazing. I looked for Pleiades – found it high in the sky over the blue jay maple tree. Suddenly there was the most brilliant shooting star traveling from right to left just under the Pleiades! When I got back inside the house the time was 2:25, making it close to 2:20 when I saw the shooting star … a Maiaspirit moment that made me feel incredible love."

Coincidentally, Brian had written the following poem just a few nights before:

Looked into Pleiades
And saw your star
Standing on its own
But a gathering nonetheless
A hug and a kiss
A shrug and wink
"about that…"
You say
Luv ya right back
You live through us we live through you
Celebrate your life from night til mornin'
The power is evident
The channel is hard
We keep moving on
Perseverance but patient

We hate the pain
We love your touch
Your spirit lives on

Another amusingly lighthearted Maiaspirit moment came later that night in Myrtle Beach. We were all together and at Mitch's request were playing a game of Hearts. The object of the game is to dump your hearts and other high point cards (e.g., Queen of Spades) onto other players and be the player with the least amount of points. We decided to play until midnight or until someone broke 100, whichever came first.

Well, poor Brian was the one getting dumped on and Mitch, the birthday boy, seemed to be getting "all the good hands." During what turned out to be the last play of the game, Lori inadvertently gave Brian the Queen of Spades, putting him well over 100 to end the game. Coincidentally, it was also midnight (the end of 11/11) and Mitch, one of Maia's closest uncles, won with an exact score of **20**.

A couple days later, the three of us (Mitch, Lori, and Brian) drove back up north and experienced two very special Maiaspirit moments.

The first occurred after Brian unknowingly selected a CD from Mitch's collection which had some special significance to Mitch and Maia. The CD contained the song "Sugar Mountain" which he had introduced to Maia the last time they were together in Sedona. As the song played, Brian felt a deep pull and sadness in his heart. The sadness lasted only a short time because right at that moment he noticed a big green sea turtle decal on the back of the car next to us … Maia?

The second entailed a most spectacular event which occurred right after Lori ended her driving shift at a Maryland rest stop.

Lori: "While the guys go in to use the rest rooms and get some coffee, I stay outside to enjoy the colors of the setting sun. Suddenly I notice a HUGE flock of birds flying southwest through the sky. When Mitch and Brian come out, we all stand for about 20 minutes in awe of this incredible sight – literally thousands of birds, perhaps 100 thousand or more, migrating in a river-like pattern that stretched far across the sky. The next day I do some internet searching and contact the local Audubon Society 'help desk.' Turns out that these birds were most likely STARlings ……. of course. ☺"

It was like we were on a roll and the signs just kept coming. For example, we had only been home for a few days when Lori makes a curious discovery related to an old pendulum clock she had inherited from her grandparents many years ago. Although the clock had never really worked, we had always kept it hanging on the wall because it was so neat to look at. Today, 11/17, Lori notices that the hands of the clock are stopped at **2:20**. Neither of us, nor Sean, had touched the clock in years, and it was almost always hidden behind an open door whenever we had company. How long the hands had been in that position, we really can't say but that's how they'll be forever more.

On Thanksgiving, since Sean had already headed to Texas for an extended visit before Julia and George's wedding, we spent the day alone together. It was actually a perfect arrangement. The day was on the mild side so we packed a picnic lunch and headed out for a four-hour hike along the nearby Wachusett Reservoir. Stopping for lunch, we sat by the water to eat our sandwiches. Just as we were finished we heard the familiar squawk of blue jays – four had decided to serenade us as we headed back home.

Dinner was pretty untraditional, but at the last minute Lori decided to make one of Maia's favorite Thanksgiving side dishes – mashed sweet potatoes baked with marshmallows on top. Unfortunately we only had two small yams so we mixed them with a few white potatoes, and fortunately we did have an old opened bag of marshmallows (probably from our Maia birthday celebration in August). Lori couldn't believe it when she counted the marshmallows – exactly **20**.

Down south in the great state of Texas, Sean and his cousins, Damon and Devon, and his Aunt Michele and Uncle Tom were having their own Maiaspirit adventure. Wanting to add an opportunity for reflection and spirituality to the day, Michele and Tom arranged for the five of them to hike up Enchanted Rock, a very ancient and sacred site near Austin. At the top they took a few moments to share some thoughts about Maia. Tom gave everyone a Sri Sai Flora incense stick and just as they were being lit, a powerful cold front from the north started to blow in. Winds picked up, temperatures dropped, and all the incense blew out. The "Maia Norther" will remain a delightful Thanksgiving memory for all our years to come.

On Friday, Nov. 26, we headed to the airport for our big trip to Texas. Love, sadness, joy, anxiety, and a whole host of other emotions swirled around us during these first few hours. Fortunately, the heaviness soon dissolved when we suddenly noticed a GIGANTIC number **20** (signifying our gate) hanging from the airport ceiling – surprisingly, neither of us had noticed this important coincidence before then. To further lighten the mood, one of our fellow passengers, a young girl who looked to be in junior high, turned her back toward us which enabled us to see a giant **20** on her sweatshirt. When she turned around again, we saw the word SPIRIT written in very large letters, surrounded by some smaller print probably describing her school. We couldn't help but smile.

We arrived in San Antonio around 8 p.m. and connected first with Brian's brother David, his daughter, Coya, and Brian's father. Later that night, we checked into our hotel and had a little time with Sean, Damon, and Michele before retiring. We didn't want to stay up too late knowing that we would need a good night's sleep to help us through the coming day. For as much as we were trying to transform any pain we felt into unconditional joy for Julia and George, we knew that this would not be easy.

Heading to bed, Lori noticed right away a beautiful 3' x 3' yellow rose print on the wall. Not really all that surprising considering that the yellow rose is the Texas state flower, but still another reassuring reminder of Maia's continual presence. As it turned out, all of us McDermott family members staying at this hotel had large yellow rose prints in our bedrooms, and though it might be true for all the hotel's bedrooms, we were all still very amused and comforted by this coincidence.

The outdoor wedding ceremony was planned to begin at 5:30 so we arrived a little after 5. Feeling nervous and uncertain as to how we would really make it through, we tried our best not to let on. Family members greeted us with sympathetic hugs and words of encouragement. Damon and Sean were handing out programs, inviting guests to write personal notes to Julia and George, and ushering folks to their seats.

Lori: "It was all so beautiful but I could feel myself trembling and fought to hold back tears. Just as we arrived, Damon pointed out a lovely photo of Maia and Julia displayed on a table with photos of other family members whose presence would be in spirit only. At that sight a few tears did escape and I really began to doubt the wisdom in coming."

Eventually we made it to our seats, sitting in the last row just in case either one of us should begin to lose it. In the time before the ceremony started we looked through the wedding program. Names of the bride's and groom's parents, officiant, wedding party, and readers on the first page, order of service on the second and third pages, and on the fourth page, beneath the "thank you" to parents, family, and friends, the following acknowledgement to "Those We Remember":

"There are many special people who are unable to be with us. The candles that surround us tonight represent the light that those people have been in our lives. And – if you happen to see those flames flicker – it has nothing to do with the wind. It is those loved ones dancing for joy at the happiness of this occasion."

On the last page was this beautiful tribute written by Julia:

Poem for Maia

Maia my light
Your flash of spirit keeps me moving
Maia my light
Your life is my own allegory for Carpe Diem
Maia my friend
You were always welcoming and warm
Maia my friend
You would have flown to me if I had asked
Maia my family
You were linked to me by blood, but we were connected by spirit
Maia my family
You will always be my boa swirling buddy
Maia my Angel
I know you are here with me now
Maia my Angel
I think about you always, miss you everyday, and love you every moment

The ceremony was lovely - filled with meaningful readings and rituals, a few moments of lighthearted humor, and palpable expressions of love for the bride and groom. We were totally reassured that our decision to attend was without a doubt the right one.

During the reception that followed, the joy and gaiety of the event was contagious. Perhaps it was as much the wine as the happy energy that surrounded us, but whatever it was, we found ourselves swept to the dance floor for a couple of songs. First Lori and Sean, then the two of us together.

And although we had earlier given ourselves permission not to dance if we weren't in the mood, we could not have held back even if we had tried.

Lori: "Upon reflecting on this a little more, I now think that what swept us onto the dance floor was Maia, inspiring us forward so that, through us, she could actually be 'dancing for joy at the happiness of this occasion'."

Maia may not have been with us in flesh and blood, but she was definitely with us, and everyone else, during this very special gathering.

Talking with other family members during those couple of days, it is clear that her death has had a huge impact. In some ways it has made us more aware of the inevitable transience of life, encouraging each of us to cherish the moments we have together and to sweat the small stuff less and less. In other ways her death has forced many of us to confront our beliefs regarding death and the possibility of "life after life," and perhaps modify them or at least get us to consider the possibility of alternative experiences.

Most importantly, however, it seems that her death has inspired us to more deeply consider the meaning and purpose of our own lives – what we do each day, how we relate to others, how we handle the cards that are dealt us and the plays that we make. What is it that we want to leave as our legacy when the time comes to take that last breath?

Lots of questions, no easy answers, and so very much to think about.

December

As the final month of 2010 begins to unfold we find ourselves at a multifaceted crossroads. Work-wise, Brian is facing the very real possibility of changing jobs at the end of the school year. A difficult job under normal circumstances, being a school district superintendent with the professional and personal challenges he's had to deal with has been practically impossible and keeps getting worse. It's clear that something needs to change but it's by no means clear what, how, or even when.

Personally, while we are amazed how far we've come since 2/20, we often wonder how we will ever manage to keep going. At times the thought of a long term future without the flesh & blood daughter we so carefully nurtured for 21 years still seems unbearable. And without personal role models to show us how to do this "staying connected in spirit" thing, we often feel like our "keep on going, see what happens" philosophy is not much to count on.

As a result, we were not too happy to welcome December or 2011 and truly wished we could just stop time long enough to figure everything out … Not to be, of course, so onward into December we went and good thing we did, because a few more very special Maiaspirit moments unfolded before us.

12/10: Lori receives a packet from her friend Gloria with information about a November candle lighting tradition held at her church to remember people who have died. For a small donation, church members can designate individual luminaries to be lit in honor of anyone they want. Gloria and another church member (whose own daughter had passed just over a year earlier) each lovingly and thoughtfully sponsored one for Maia. Of the 119 luminaries lit this year, the numbers for Maia's luminaries were 51 and 95. Adding 5 + 1 + 9 + 5 we get …… **20**.

12/17: Lori finalizes the guest list for a low-key surprise birthday celebration for Brian. Beginning with an invitation list of 18 people, two people can't come, and two people ask to bring four more. 18 − 2 + 4 = **20.**

Also today Lori gets an email from Kesshi, the daughter of one of her best friends: *"Hi Lori, just stopping by to say that I love you. I saw a Carpe Diem sign while walking around Rome. Then it started pouring. :)"*

The most amazing Maiaspirit moments occur on 12/18, Brian's birthday. Knowing that this could be a tough day for both of us, we make a 1:00 p.m. appointment with Pamela Landenburg, a spiritual medium working in Westford, a town about 30 minutes from Clinton. We had wanted to experience the work of another medium for comparison purposes anyway and today just seemed like the perfect time.

The appointment was held at a holistic/new age book store in Westford. We arrived a little early so we would have some time to browse around the store. As soon as we parked the car and started walking toward the store entrance, we heard a familiar squawk - two blue jays having a little fun in a nearby spruce tree.

Unfortunately, the session starts off a little slow – we are not connecting much to anything Pamela is saying. But after about five minutes she starts getting an image of a young woman with dark, shiny hair and beautiful white sparkling teeth … Maia?

Pamela: *She's making me feel like she was very grateful for the time that she spent here. She's saying that she had a very strong support system, that there was so much love. She's flashing me what looks like the Star of David … do you understand this? … She's saying that she always had these times of getting weak, then she'd have these spurts of energy to where it looked very hopeful and then things would go back and she said it was a struggle all the time and it was like life was playing a game on her. One minute she was well, the next minute she was feeling strong, and then the next minute she would get weak again. It was back and forth, and back and forth, and she's saying that she doesn't know what she would have ever done without her family. She's also making me feel like she had some really good friends.*

She's saying 'a lot of people didn't understand' and she's going on about circumstances, that some things just happened and these were my circumstances. My energy was up and down and up and down, and I'm getting a lot in my head … do you understand the head? … She doesn't want anyone to think that she didn't appreciate things, 'cause she feels so gracious and grateful to me. She feels like, when she was here, others felt like she didn't appreciate things and that this is how she felt. That people thought she took advantage of things, that this is how people saw her.

Do you understand the sparkles of light? Pay attention to the sparkles of light. This is how she shows herself, little sparkles of light.

She says she's very strong, she says she's very at peace, she's very much around. She's going to some type of a drink. She's making me feel like it's some kind of wine and it's making my lips feel tingly. It's a light red color. I'm tasting it and it doesn't taste like an alcoholic beverage to me, it tastes very sweet ... now I'm feeling very relaxed so it must have been wine or champagne. I'm not a drinker. It tastes very flat, there are no bubbles in it. But she's going, she wants me to go to you (Lori), like this is something that you need to have.

But now she's going to you (Brian) and I'm tasting a lot of pastries ... very light, almost like a sugar cookie but it's not a sugar cookie. Do you like sweets? ... And she's showing me ... do you bake? She's showing me rolling something, and I'm tasting a little chocolate it's almost like, whatever she's showing me, I'm tasting hazel nut in there. And she's showing me drizzling, the chocolate drizzling. And she's giving you a round of applause, like you've made some progress with that ... baking?

She's making me feel like the both of you need to have an outlet. There's a lot of emotional stuff going on right now and she's making me feel like there's something you can learn from, kind of to let this go. She's also showing me a lot of pottery, too. And she's showing me a picture. She's making me feel like someone has a picture of her and there's either a light or a candle in front of it, it's all lit up. She's saying thank you.

She's making me, I'm not sure who she is to you yet, but she's making me feel like she had no idea how much she was cared about by the both of

you when she was here. And again she's saying that it was how she felt. I can't say that she was negative 'cause she feels like she was a beautiful soul to me, but when she was here she didn't see things for what they were. She always kind of saw the opposite of what other people saw of her …

And she's showing me a floral arrangement now. It's very big. What's she focusing on? She's telling me there's something that swirls in it. Do you understand this?

Brian: *In the flower arrangement?*

Pamela: *Yeah, there's something inside of it that has little swirls to it.*

Lori: *A birthday bouquet? (Lori bought flowers for Brian's birthday.)*

Brian's birthday bouquet.

Pamela: *She's going on about how much she loves the sparkles. If she could only have seen all this beauty while she was here.*

She's going on about how she had blinders on and she's going on about writing, writing. There's something in her story, the story of her life, that can help other people, and she's making me feel like someone's going to be writing about her life, and going out and helping other people with her story. I see someone talking in a group, it looks like a woman. I can't figure out who this is. I'm getting the chills right now. She's making me feel like she's all excited by this. I don't see this as something that's going to happen soon, I feel like it's something that's going to happen in the future. I feel like someone is starting to think about doing some kind of intervention with people. But she's getting very, very excited about this ...

She's showing me a dog, a little dog. When I see a little white dog, this means loyalty and she wants to thank you for that. But she's also showing me a smaller dog that she has with her. She's very excited .... She's making me feel like this animal had some type of medical problems and passed away before its time and she's showing me how much life this pet has right now. It's licking her and she's very excited that she's still here and that this is her little companion ...

Lori: *Penny!*

Our dog, Penny, who died of kidney disease before her sixth birthday.

Pamela: *She's showing me candles and she wants to say thank you. Someone's been lighting candles for her and I see a lot of tears. And she's making me feel like this person, whoever it was, was very afraid of 'where is she? Where is she going?' And she wants you to know that she's still right here. And she's going on about heaven and hell. Was she very confused about religion stuff when she was here? 'Cause she's telling me 'it's non-existent, I'm very happy, I'm still a part of everybody and it's beautiful here. It's beautiful. I can see things in a different light now and I can visit whoever I want whenever I want and it's just a beautiful place. I feel so much peace and my heart is full of so much love. I couldn't feel these things when I was here but I am so happy now and I can help you, I can help you'* …

She's also showing me a turtle that's walking and then stops, and turns into stone. So with this I have to say, turtles bring in a lot of peace in the family and also prosperity on many levels. So she's showing me this turtle that walks in, turns to stone, so there's going to be a lot of abundance, peace, and extra cash coming in this year. She's saying that you both worked very hard - you understand? - and she's making me feel like you held back on your life a little bit. And this is your time to be free and live and she's going to be with you every step of the way. She's showing me both of you having fun especially you (Lori) you're just like a child all over again. And she's saying that this is how she wants you to be. There's a lot of happiness coming up and she's never going to leave your side …

She's making me feel like there's a lot of healing coming in as well, not just within yourself, I feel like you're going to be helping lots of other people to heal. She's making me feel like your whole thought process is changing on how you look at things now and she's making me feel like you really believe in your own power to heal. You understand? I'm seeing hands. What is this green … green? Green represents healing. She's showing me a lot of green. It also represents money but I feel like there's a lot of healing to be done …

She's saying that she never understood people and 'in the place where I'm at now I do. I can see straight through and I can understand people now and I can understand their hearts. And I can understand how people don't think when they speak' and she's actually saying that she likes the place where she's at because she can be of more assistance. She felt like she was a burden when she was here. She knows now that she wasn't but that's how she felt when she was here. She wants you to look at her now as your guide and protector. She's saying that things have changed a lot for you both and she's saying that things have gotten better if you open your eyes and see. She says she'll always take care of you and she knows that you could never do anything wrong 'cause she'll always be guiding you. Is this your daughter? 'Cause she's making me feel like she's saying she doesn't know how you got me 'cause she's making me feel her personality isn't anything like either one of you. But she was always very grateful and wishes she could have seen things then the way she sees things now, but that she couldn't, but now she knows that she can help you and that you deserve so much now and what you were going through just a few years ago …

She says she's fine. She's feeling so much peace and she's very much a part of your life. And she likes how you still do things for her but she wants to do something for you. And she says she's working at it. She's still by your side. She's really stressing that 'I'm more of an assistance to you now than I was when I was here.' She's really, again, she says sorry 'cause she's making me feel like she really felt like she held you back. This is just how she felt when she was here - she feels like she serves you more purposefully now …

She's showing me someone pinning pictures up, making a collage of some sort. She's saying she really loves it. But again she's going to someone painting and she's showing me someone painting a picture of her. She says she was very artistic, like she was but didn't work at it. She's making me feel like she's going to work through you, you understand? Oh my, she's going on about spirit artists. Have you ever been? And she's making me feel like this is what you're going to be doing some day …

She wants me to give you this (deck of fairy oracle cards). Do you have any questions for her? She just keeps saying she's going to be around you, she's going to be helping you so much, you can feel her. (To Brian) You're not feeling her as much though because you're not sure how you feel yet. (To Lori) You're a little bit more open …Here, shuffle these (fairy cards) please …

Did someone write a prayer for her? She's making me feel like there was a prayer written exclusively for her, like somebody made this up while thinking of her … She's saying that she loves it. She's making me feel like they should be in books, to help others. She's really concerned about helping others and this is what you're going to be doing. That will be her legacy, she says and she's laughing and she's saying 'I really love it, I really love it and I wish I could have seen things differently when I was here but I was here for a purpose.'

(To Brian) I want you to take three of them (fairy cards). She's also going on about how she didn't mean to take anything from you, and what I'm feeling when she's saying this is that, by her going and leaving you, she didn't mean to take so much from you … Hmm … (about the cards) Does any of this make sense? (Birthday, New Home, Summer)

Brian: *Today's my birthday.*

Pamela: *Is it? Oh, happy birthday. Do you understand the New Home and Summer? She's making me feel like, do you understand where she's saying it's OK to move? She's making me feel like there's too much pain and the memories there and that she wants you to only stay with the happy memories and that it's OK, you're not going to be leaving her behind. Wherever you go is where she'll be.*

And she's also going on about this star … It's almost like 'this star that someone pointed out as being me and this is where I am and this is where you can connect with me, when you look at the star you'll feel me more.'

Pamela *(begins to shuffle cards): She's saying 'I love you both so much and I didn't want to hurt you'… (one of the cards pops out of the deck) …and she's actually saying that you're going to be moving along, not without her, she'll be by your side every step of the way and your life is going to be beautiful and extremely happy. And she keeps focusing on the work you're going to do to help others and she keeps saying 'cause you're not stuck and you're going to help the people who are stuck.*

Pamela *(looking at the three cards that popped out – Daughter, Spiritual Teacher, Everything's OK): Now this is pretty much what she's been saying, that you're going to be helping others, you're going to be teaching, and that with the spirit artist I really feel like that's something that you're going to be doing and with her help.*

She's saying 'I love you and I'll always be by your side' and she's also focusing on clouds, somebody keeps seeing signs in the clouds from her, and she's saying 'just know, just know I'm always going to be around and I'm going to be helping you. And I love you very much' and again she says she's sorry, she's sorry and she's very proud of you and she loves you. She's showing me sheer curtains just blowing …

She's making me feel like you're doing a really good job and with the writing, she's making me feel like you're just going to write, like she's coming right through you and helping you. With the signs, you're just going to write everything down and you'll know when it's her and when it's not. You'll get that feeling, ok? … I really don't think there's anything much anyone can teach you. Just know that it is her and channeling guides is not really necessary 'cause you're working with her directly in spirit. … Just talk to her, they communicate telepathically but there are some times when you won't feel like she's around 'cause they do have other things to do on the other side as well. But I feel like she is going to be doing a lot of things with you, like channeling writings, and paintings, just know ... sometimes you can feel her right next to you, like she's just there.

Brian: *How do we do what you're doing?*

Pamela: *Just do it ... But you need to heal first before you can help others. Learn to accept that this is your relationship with your daughter now. You still have the relationship; it's just a little bit different now. And once you get past that then you can help others and you just go with it. I think you do need to have faith in a higher power than yourself. Exploring other tools, runes, can also be good ... Right now I think the best thing for you is to keep doing what you're doing ... Just experiencing your daughter's energy... She's giving you a lot of guidance.*

When the session was over, we got back into our car (no blue jays squawking) and headed back home. Another extraordinary experience to think about, try to make sense of, and to help us find direction on this ever unpredictable "MFM Magical Mystical Journey."

Two very unusual events occur a few days later. First, Lori has an early morning dream in which she's with Tina, a former colleague and friend who she hasn't seen in many months. While walking to work a few hours later, quite unexpectedly she and Tina just happen to cross paths.

The second event occurs later that afternoon while Lori is transcribing the voice recording from our session with Pamela.

Lori: "When Brian gets home from work, probably around 6, he brings me a glass of wine. Unlike the dark red wines we usually drink, this wine is light red, a leftover from his birthday celebration. Unbeknownst to him, I am <u>right at that exact moment</u> transcribing the part where Pamela is talking about a light red drink, probably wine, and saying that Maia wants me to have it. ... pretty astonishing timing I'd say."

Later that night Brian writes the following in our journal:

"I couldn't 'say' it then (3/2010) and I still have a hard time accepting – but – someday we will look back and say this changed us forever and for the better. Too hard to say/think/feel (now).... Maia, you have already changed every part of our being and we count on you to keep teaching us, guiding us, and (most important) being with us – Luv ya"

12/22: Brian's sister Michele sends us and Sean the following "Maia Memory" email:

"Not long after Devon arrived home from NY I saw her frantically searching the kitchen shelf where we keep our recipe books. 'I can't find it!' She was looking for the magazine she had gotten from a craft store last year that had the cookie recipes she and Maia used. I said 'we have other cookbooks with cookie recipes.'

Devon stopped searching and faced all of us. 'NO. When I couldn't get any of the dough to come out right and was getting frustrated, NO ONE helped me except Maia!'

Maia jumped in and figured out how to fold the dough and place the cherries to make lovely Poinsettia flowers and put the parts of the Santa Clauses together just right. And when Devon was up to her elbows in marshmallow dough goop and about to lose it, Maia's presence at her side made her laugh hysterically and then we all laughed at their mess and silliness together.

The four of us laughed together at that memory, and then we hugged in turns and dried each other's tears as we thanked Maia for bringing joy to our lives last Christmas. We will never make Christmas cookies without laughter and love for Maia in our hearts.

P.S. The next time Devon looked on the shelf, the recipe book was right in front of her... Maia?"

In response, Sean writes back:

"Thanks so much for this Michele! Once again this proves that Maia will always be with us in our memories and what she has taught (and is still teaching) us. When you're up to your elbows in goop and are about to lose it, sometimes you just need to realize how silly life is and laugh about it!"

12/23: Two of Maia's best Clinton friends, Felicia and Michelle, stop by for a visit. They were by our side every day for the first week after Maia's passing. They have been in touch with us regularly since then, stopping by when they're in town, sending emails and text messages about silly things and Maiaspirit moments, and we love them like daughters.

That night they come bearing gifts: two TexMex style coffee mugs with matching shot glasses. Written inside the card which accompanied these special gifts was a note: *"To start and end your days correctly, the way she would!"*

The following morning, Lori is enjoying some coffee in the Kokopelli mug she had just been given and takes another look at the card. Unnoticed last night was the illustration on the front of the card: seven star-shaped cookies, just like the seven major stars in the Pleiades constellation. She contacts Felicia and Michelle to find out if this was intentional on their part … "No," they reply, "we had no idea."

12/26: Lori makes the following final journal entry for 2010:

I AM THE DRAGONSPIRIT

Dragons don't die.

Epilogue

Today is February 13, 2011, one week away from celebrating the first anniversary of Maia's passing.

Although we cannot imagine feeling "celebratory" in the traditional sense, we will try our best to signify this day with great joy and pride for our Maia. We will recommit ourselves to living life as she would, with compassion and carpe diem, and to letting her spirit, amazing, awe-inspiring Maiaspirit, live on through our thoughts and deeds.

We will no doubt feel sadness, for we miss her so very, very much. But we do not want sorrow to color the day. Rather, we will try to adorn it in yellows and pinks, music and friendship, smiles, happy memories, and, perhaps, speculations as to what the next chapter of this post-220 journey may have in store, for both Maia and for us.

Her passing still pains us deeply. Perhaps it always will, or maybe not … we certainly are no longer confident in anyway to predict the future. What used to be impossible, no longer is. What used to seem like a terrible fate, no longer does. Animals speak, coincidence matters, and we live in a universe that reason alone can't understand. With patience and perseverance, we will just have to keep on going and see what happens.

To all who are learning to dance with us on this incredible journey - we cannot say thank you enough for loving Maia and loving us. Your support, encouragement, and humorous companionship have been, and will continue to be, so very important.

To our most beloved Maia – our sincerest apologies for anything we should have done that we didn't and anything that we did do that we shouldn't have, both during your years here on this earth with us and from 2/20 on. We love you more than words can ever say. You have always been our sparkling light, our dragon, our turtle, and our bee, our Maia-bo-baia and shining star, our teacher and our yellow rose. Now and forever, you will be all of those and so very much more, for one thing does seem certain:

Dragons don't die. They get stronger.

About the Authors

Lori and Brian McDermott are both educators who met in 1982 while attending graduate school at Texas A&M University. They moved to Massachusetts in 1988 with their two children, Sean and Maia, and continue to live and work in the central Massachusetts area.

Brian, Maia, Sean, & Lori McDermott
December 27, 2009
(San Antonio, Texas)

Appendices

Excerpts from Maia's Memorial Service

I   Welcome: Loni Feinberg

Psalm 121

I will lift my eyes to the mountains. What is the source of my help? The source of my help is the One, Creator of heaven and earth. The One will not let you falter; your Guardian does not slumber. Surely the Guardian of all neither slumbers nor sleeps. The One is at your right hand to protect you, the One, your Keeper, gives shelter. The sun will not smite you by day, nor the moon by night. The One will guard you from all harm. The One will preserve your soul and will guard your going and coming from this time forth and forever.

So, what are we doing here? I choose my words carefully in this question.

I come from a tradition where when a group of newly freed slave-people were receiving unfathomable enlightenment at the bottom of a desert mountain, their response was Na-ah-seh v'nishmah: We will do and we will hear. Notice the order of things in that response. First we'll **do** and then we'll try to hear.

We're approaching the end of a 7 day period – another unfathomable time. During this week, what I heard from so many people, including myself, were the questions: What do I do? What do I do now? What should we do next? What can we do to help? Tell me what to do.

So, right now, we are going to work together to do two things. First, we are going to collectively continue to reach out to Maia through the porous veil which separates where we are now from where she is now, and we're going to support her soul in its journey. We will do this through our voices, our thoughts, our words, our prayers.

Second, we will begin the process of bringing the world, which is terribly off-balance right now, back into balance. We will do this by sharing our memories of and love for Maia and transforming them from their purpose a week ago, to their purpose from now on. That is, we transform these feelings and memories from a purpose of informing how we would interact with Maia the next time we saw her or spoke to her, to using those memories to inform how we will interact with each and every person going forward. The power of that, coming from this many people, is awe inspiring.

I know there are many teachers and educators here today, who would tell me that proper teaching pedagogy dictates that I should give an example. So here's my example.

Sometime this week, Lori and I were together in a corner, and Lori told me of something she had learned from Maia. Speaking about herself, Lori said that she tends to load everything she does with a dose of intense seriousness. One time, when she was in the throes of acting out one of these self-serious episodes Maia said to her mother, "Lighten up. It'll be alright."

We will start by hearing a Poem for Maia from John McDermott, Maia's grandfather, who wrote this on the occasion of her birth. Note that after some music and words from members of Maia's family, we will call upon anyone who would like to say a few words to come up to do so. For those whose hearts just got stuck in their throats at the thought of speaking now in front of all these people, lighten up. Don't feel you have to do this now. There will be ample opportunity to share your thoughts at any time in any way. It's a lifelong process.

II   Poem for Maia: John J. McDermott

Prologue: February 26, 2010
Coming in the midst of an atrocious three years in the lives of the Texas McDermott family, the birth of Maia was a tumblefull of grace that bathed and balmed our sorrows. Today, sorrowful once more, we return to her presence for help, for healing, once again.

Maia Felisse

Sistering Sean
Will be no
Easy task
Yet, little one
Your eyes

Say that I, me
Come to
play
Among the potteried
Computers
Which dot the
Intriguing landscape
Of your domestic
Presence
Your nominal origins
Are of
The flight to the
Golden land
M. is for Mary
As in
Aveta
F. is for Frank
As in Picarelli
A canvas bag
Refracted by the
Hoot
Of the New York
Ferry
Ellis Islanding
One's way to a new
Start
A winding, painful, joyful
Route
From Riginell
To Brian and Lori
Italy and Israel
Prima Diva and Shofar
How rich
How America
You are, however,
Native Texan
Yet, a journey, for you
To the first
Commonwealth,
Massachusetts by name
To become a Yankee,

Egad!
And so, fat of cheek
Rich of skin
You become as a
Symbol of Peace
An Exodus into
The Zion of
Human affection
One of many …
James Douglas
Julia Lynne
Sean Robert
Maia Felisse
Number four
As they say,
More to come
Damon Carey
Devon Michele
Coya Virginia
As you flood
the middle
Of this new generation
Welcome.

Epilogue:
And, for today,
And for all
Of our tomorrows
Never, ever
Goodbye.

III   Song for Maia: Loni

I now invite you to join in a Song for Maia. This is a chant Lori learned and loves from the group Libana. The melody is borrowed from the Native American tradition. We will be using Maia's name for the words.

Maia: ancient Roman Goddess of springtime, warmth and increase; in Greek mythology, the eldest of the Pleiades, the seven daughters of Atlas and Pleione.

Felisse: Latin for happy.

We'll start by taking a few minutes to learn the melody ... And then I'll explain how we will chant together .... Mainly, though, focus on Maia Felisse.

IV Reflections: Lori, Brian, & Sean

Lori:
Becoming a parent has been the most important experience in my life but one for which there was no all encompassing "how to" book or definitive family tradition. As a result I found myself learning a lot through trial and error, reading various books on assorted topics, and often just making it up as we went along. This being said, the following excerpt from Kahlil Gibran's The Prophet, which I first encountered as a 21 year old college kid, set the tone and remains true today.

And a woman who held a babe against her bosom said, "Speak to us of Children." And he said:

Your children are not your children.
They are the sons and daughters of Life's longing for itself.
They come through you but not from you,
And though they are with you yet they belong not to you.

You may give them your love but not your thoughts,
For they have their own thoughts.
You may house their bodies but not their souls,
For their souls dwell in the house of tomorrow,
which you cannot visit, not even in your dreams.
You may strive to be like them,
but seek not to make them like you.
For life goes not backward nor tarries with yesterday.

Maia was born in 1988, which according to the Chinese Zodiac is the Year of The Dragon, the mightiest of all the zodiac signs. Dragons symbolize such character traits as dominance and ambition. Dragons prefer to live by their own rules and if left on their own, are usually successful. They are driven, unafraid of challenges, and willing to take risks. They are passionate in all they do and they do things in grand fashion, traits which, unfortunately, can also leave Dragons feeling exhausted and curiously unfulfilled. Dragons get along well with other ambitious signs like the Rat or Monkey.

I was born in 1958, the Year of the Dog, symbolized by traits such as loyalty, getting along with others, and kindness. Dogs like to finish what they start, spend money wisely, and like well-kept organized houses. Most importantly, Dogs are extremely _in_compatible with Dragons.

Being the mother Dog to a daughter Dragon prophetically ensured that life with Maia would be both wonderful and challenging, and so it has been. From the very beginning her passion for life was obvious, her love of people unquestionable, and, much to my chagrin, her need to live by her own rules unrelenting. Those of us who know Maia can relate that there has never been a limit she didn't test or a mandate she didn't challenge.

For the past twenty one and a half years and on into the future, Maia has been and will continue to be one of my greatest joys, my most enigmatic puzzle, and in so many ways, my greatest teacher. Leading by example, she's taught me how to embrace life and people, find fun and let loose, and that doing something for someone who needs you, even when it's not convenient, is worth it no matter what. And, perhaps most importantly, she's taught me that there are no obstacles when you care strongly enough.

In closing, I'd like to read another excerpt from <u>The Prophet</u>.

THEN Almitra spoke, saying, "We would ask now of Death." And he said:

You would know the secret of death.
But how shall you find it unless you seek it in the heart of life?
The owl whose night-bound eyes are blind unto the day cannot unveil the mystery of light.
If you would indeed behold the spirit of death, open your heart wide unto the body of life. For life and death are one, even as the river and the sea are one.

In the depth of your hopes and desires lies your silent knowledge of the beyond;

And like seeds dreaming beneath the snow your heart dreams of spring.
Trust the dreams, for in them is hidden the gate to eternity.

Your fear of death is but the trembling of the shepherd when he stands before the
king whose hand is to be laid upon him in honour.
Is the shepherd not joyful beneath his trembling, that he shall wear the mark of
the king?
Yet is he not more mindful of his trembling?

For what is it to die but to stand naked in the wind and to melt into the sun?
And what is it to cease breathing, but to free the breath from its restless tides, that
it may rise and expand and seek God unencumbered?

Only when you drink from the river of silence shall you indeed sing.
And when you have reached the mountain top, then you shall begin to climb.
And when the earth shall claim your limbs, then shall you truly dance.

Brian:
Many people have talked about how Maia "filled whatever room she was in"
- clearly she is here with us because she filled this one as well. Thank you all
for your wonderful support, love, and friendship.

I don't know how to do this and I suppose that's a good thing… I won't take
much time, not because I don't have so, so much to share about Maia, but
because I just don't know how to do this….

It has been 7 days and throughout all of this very tumultuous and painful
time only one thing has been easy to do, answer the question about what kind
of flowers we should have at this service.

Pink and Yellow Roses.

Pink and yellow were two of Maia's favorite colors. As was shared in Maia's
poem, she was born in Texas and so the yellow rose provides a connection to
her birthplace and beginnings. And anybody who knows Maia knows that
pink played a very big role in her life.

So many people describe Maia as an amazingly beautiful and strong woman.
And certainly she was. She stood firm and, like the strength of the long
stem rose, held her ground and kept her presence known. Her beauty was

unmistakable from birth and as years passed her blossom became more and more exquisite.

Many of you also know that Maia could be as sharp and piercing as the most intense thorn on the largest rose you could find.

But only those who really know Maia also know that Maia was as fragile as the most delicate rose petal. She carried the burden of her friends, of strangers and would do anything to help a troubled soul. But Maia did not carry her own burdens well and her petals often fell and her pain went deep.

Nevertheless, as with our Pink and Yellow roses, Maia made sure that people knew of her strength, her thorn, and her beauty and that's how we remember our amazing Maia.

We have received so many flowers from all of our wonderful family and friends and not surprisingly, many of them were pink and yellow roses.

We will always love you and learn from you, our beloved Maia.

Sean:
Saturday morning at 5:38am my mom left a message on my phone saying just that I needed to call back right away. From her voice's tone alone, I knew it could only be about my father or Maia. When I called back and my father answered, amidst a thousand thoughts rushing through my head I became emotionally stalled.

I had felt that I should have been able to do something for Maia, though I knew there was nothing. I knew I had to be able to get my parents through this but I didn't know what to do. I didn't know how to act. And I didn't know if what I was feeling was how I was supposed to feel. I knew that my own way of coping, my sense of reason, was insufficient for them, as there is no reason for a loss that hurts this much. All I knew, all I understood was that my mother and father are trying to endure something that no parent should ever go through. I was consumed with the full understanding that I can never truly empathize with their pain, and they became my only concern and I came home immediately.

Those who know me could say I often try to find a positive that goes along with every negative. It took a few days but as more and more friends and phone calls flowed support, warmth, and love through our home I started to see it. I never before realized how powerful it all was, but your love for my parents, myself, and most importantly for Maia is our only way of conquering the insurmountable. Despite having to undeservedly bear the weight of an inconceivable tragedy, my family and I have been tremendously blessed with friends who would, and have, done everything and more for us. We could never do it without you and hope you know that we would do anything and everything for you in a heartbeat. Just like Maia would. Thank you all so much.

V   A Gaelic Blessing: Composed by John Rutter; Sung by Billy & Mary Walsh

Deep peace of the running wave to you ...

Deep peace of Christ to you

VI   Reflections: Family and Friends

VII   Mourner's Kaddish

Oh God, Full of Compassion, You who dwell on high, grant perfect rest beneath the sheltering wings of Your Presence, among the holy and pure who shine as the brightness on the heavens, unto the soul of Maia Felisse, daughter of Brian and Lori, sister of Sean, granddaughter, niece, cousin, friend, our Maia Felisse, who has gone unto eternity and in whose memory charity is offered. May her repose be in paradise. May the Merciful One bring her under the cover of the One's wings forever, and may her soul be bound up in the bond of eternal life. May the One be her possession, and may she rest in peace. Amen.

Please open your programs to find the Mourner's Kaddish, an ancient prayer from the Jewish tradition. It is under the picture of Maia. The group responses are in bold, but feel free to join Maia's family in reciting the entire Kaddish.

VIII Bagpipe Medley: Tom Nelson

Maia's Song

Words & Music by Giddens Rateau (February 2010)

These are the sounds of Heaven's gates opening
Angelic organs play the chords and serenade your soul
Maia Felisse McDermott, Rest In Peace

Looking in the sky, and wondering why
It's always the good when young people die
It took me by surprise, God shut my eyes
I'm trying not to cry, oh, trying not to cry
But the tears keep dripping out
Just keep flipping out
Getting phone calls that your gone, what is this about?
Been in shock before, but never in this amount
God bless your family, God Damn it, we go'n miss you. How
Could such a thing happen to a life loving spirit
Maia went to a better place, her voice I can hear it
So vividly in my mind, timidly spending time
Trying to stay strong, not crying, but it's a grind
Grind on the mind, grind on the heart
Mine is in parts, finding a spark
That will light the flame on Maia's candle forever
It will burn through the wind and any type of weather
I remember the September when I first saw your face
You met me, with a smile and a witty embrace
I asked God, why did she leave us alone?
He told me, "It was time and he needed her home"

In Heaven, She lives on (in heaven, in heaven) (she lives on, she lives on)
Angels sing, Maia's song (The angels, They're singing) (This is Maia's song)

Who can forget the times, you would see Maia
When she saw you, she'd give you a big smile
I'll tell you right now what I miss the most
Is sitting with her in class, as we laugh at her jokes
We're gonna miss her loving, energetic, personality
I can feel my pain, and the pain of her family

The pain of her friends, too much suffering
The pain of the girls in 33 Puffton
I'm huffing and puffing, no not for nothing
Anxiety attacks, it's all out of loving
All out of mourning, but no more mourning
Let's celebrate her life from night til morning
Maia's smiling down, that you can trust
God's newest angel, she lives through us

I asked God, why did she leave us alone?
He told me, "It was time and he needed her home"

In Heaven, She lives on (in heaven, in heaven) (she lives on, she lives on)
Angels sing, Maia's song (The angels, They're singing) (This is Maia's song)

http://www.youtube.com/watch?v=G4yHbrQ5gks

Bibliography

Andrews, Ted. *Animal-Speak: The Spiritual & Magical Powers of Creatures Great & Small.* St.Paul: Llewellyn Publications, 1993.

Berkowitz, Rita S. & Deborah S. Romaine. *The Complete Idiot's Guide to Communicating with Spirits.* Indianapolis: Alpha Books, 2003.

Berkus, Rusty. *To Heal Again: Towards Serenity and the Resolution of Grief.* Los Angeles: Red Rose Press, 1984.

Blum, Ralph H. *The New Book of Runes Set.* New York: St. Martins Press, 1983.

Evans-Wentz, W.Y. ed. *The Tibetan Book of the Dead: Or The After-Death Experiences on the Bardo Plane.* London: Oxford University Press, 1960.

Gibran, Kahlil. *The Prophet.* New York: Alfred A. Knopf, 1923.

Hoffman, Luellen. *Special Dreams: Personal Accounts After the Death of a Loved One.* New York: Crossroad Publishing Company, 2009.

McDermott, Robert. *The New Essential Steiner: An Introduction to Rudolf Steiner for the 21st Century.* Great Barrington: Lindisfarne Books, 2009.

McWilliams, Peter and John-Roger. *You Can't Afford the Luxury of a Negative Thought.* Los Angeles: Prelude Press, 1988.

Noble, Vicki. *Motherpeace: A Way to the Goddess Through Myth, Art, and Tarot.* New York: HarperCollins, 1994.

Schumacher, E. F. *A Guide for the Perplexed.* New York: Harper & Row Publishers, 1977.

Smith, Larry and Rachel Fershleiser. *Not Quite What I Was Planning, Revised and Expanded Deluxe Edition: Six-Word Memoirs by Writers Famous and Obscure.* New York: HarperCollins Publishers, 2008.

Steiner, Rudolph. *Staying Connected : How to Continue Your Relationships With Those Who Have Died*. Hudson: Anthroposophic Press, 1999.

Tadd, Ellen. *Death and Letting Go*. Montague: Montague Press, 2003.

Van Praagh, James. *Talking to Heaven: A Medium's Message of Life After Death*. New York: Signet Books, 1997.

Virtue, Doreen. *Magical Messages from the Fairies Oracle Cards: A 44-Card Deck and Guidebook*. Carlsbad: Hay House, Inc., 2008.

Weiss, Brian. *Many Lives, Many Masters: The True Story of a Prominent Psychiatrist, His Young Patient, and the Past-Life Therapy That Changed Both Their Lives*. New York: Simon & Schuster, Inc., 1988.

Wilhelm, Richard. *The I Ching or Book of Changes*. New York: Bollingen Foundation, Inc., 1950.

9 781452 537153